— **STABILIZING NIGERIA** —

The Center for Preventive Action's Preventive Action Reports

A series sponsored by
the COUNCIL ON FOREIGN RELATIONS and
THE CENTURY FOUNDATION,
formerly the Twentieth Century Fund

Volume I: *Toward Comprehensive Peace in Southeast Europe: Conflict Prevention in the South Balkans* (Report of the South Balkans Working Group)

Volume II: *Cases and Strategies for Preventive Action* (Papers from the Center for Preventive Action's Third Annual Conference)

Volume III: *Stabilizing Nigeria: Sanctions, Incentives, and Support for Civil Society* (Report of the Nigeria Project)

Center for Preventive Action
Council on Foreign Relations
58 East 68th Street
New York, NY 10021
tel: (212) 434-9400
fax: (212) 517-4967
www.foreignrelations.org

The Century Foundation
formerly the Twentieth Century Fund
41 East 70th Street
New York, NY 10021
tel: (212) 535-4441
fax: (212) 535-7534
www.tcf.org

To order any of the Preventive Action Reports,
please call 1 (800) 552-5450

PREVENTIVE ACTION REPORTS
VOLUME 3

STABILIZING NIGERIA

Sanctions, Incentives, and Support for Civil Society

Peter M. Lewis, Pearl T. Robinson, and Barnett R. Rubin

SPONSORED BY THE COUNCIL ON FOREIGN RELATIONS
AND THE CENTURY FOUNDATION

1998 • The Century Foundation Press • New York

THE CENTURY FOUNDATION

The Century Foundation, formerly the Twentieth Century Fund, sponsors and supervises timely analyses of economic policy, foreign affairs, and domestic political issues. Not-for-profit and nonpartisan, it was founded in 1919 and endowed by Edward A. Filene.

Library of Congress Cataloging-in-Publication Data

Lewis, Peter Michael, 1957–
    Stabilizing Nigeria : sanctions, incentives, and support for civil
society / Peter M. Lewis, Pearl T. Robinson, and Barnett R. Rubin.
        p.   cm. — (Preventive action reports ; v. 3)
    Report of the findings and recommendations of a task force established by the
Council on Foreign Relations' Center for Preventive Action (CPA).
    "Sponsored by the Council on Foreign Relations and The Century Foundation."
    Copyrighted by: the Council on Foreign Relations®, Inc.
    Includes index.
    ISBN–0–87078–415–3
    1. Nigeria—Politics and government—1984– 2. Political stability—Nigeria.
3. United States—Foreign relations—Nigeria.   4. Nigeria—Foreign relations—
United States.   I. Robinson, Pearl T., 1945–. II. Rubin, Barnett R. III. Council on
Foreign Relations.   IV. Center for Preventive Action.   V. Century Foundation.
VI. Title.   VII. Series.
DT515.842.L49   1998
320.9669—dc21
                                                                98–23151
                                                                    CIP

COUNCIL ON FOREIGN RELATIONS

The Council on Foreign Relations, Inc. is a nonprofit, nonpartisan national membership organization dedicated to promoting improved understanding of international affairs through the free and civil exchange of ideas. The Council is a forum where leaders from academia, government, business, nonprofit organizations, and the media come together to discuss the most important international issues. The goals of the Council are to find and nurture the next generation of foreign policy leaders; to contribute ideas to U.S. foreign policy and the understanding of international politics; and to reach beyond our walls with literature and broadcast programs to Americans with interest in these issues.

The Council takes no institutional position on policy issues and has no affiliation with the U.S. government. All statements of fact and expressions of opinion contained in all its publications are the sole responsibility of the authors.

For further information about the Council on Foreign Relations, please contact the Public Affairs Office, Council on Foreign Relations, 58 East 68th Street, New York, NY 10021, (212) 434–9400.

Note

The Council on Foreign Relations takes no position on issues. This document represents the views of the authors alone. The authors benefited from consultations with the Nigeria Working Group of the Center for Preventive Action, but the members of the Working Group bear no responsibility for the conclusions herein. Part I was written by Peter M. Lewis, Pearl T. Robinson, and Barnett R. Rubin. Part II was written by Lewis and Rubin.

Acknowledgments

This is the third volume in the Center for Preventive Action's Preventive Action Reports, a series that is cosponsored by The Century Foundation, formerly the Twentieth Century Fund, and the Council on Foreign Relations. This volume was made possible by the generous support of the Carnegie Corporation of New York and The Century Foundation. The Center for Preventive Action is grateful to the members of the Nigeria Working Group, to Darren Kew, who jump-started the project, to Nana-Oye Addo-Yobo for guiding the project to its fruition, and to Anya Schmemann and Susanna P. Campbell for outstanding assistance with the manuscript.

CONTENTS

━ PREFACE ━

THE CENTER FOR PREVENTIVE ACTION

Director: Barnett R. Rubin

Chair: Gen. John W. Vessey, USA (Ret.)

The Center for Preventive Action (CPA) was established by the Council on Foreign Relations in 1994 to study and test conflict prevention. CPA is chaired by General John W. Vessey, USA (Ret.), former chairman of the Joint Chiefs of Staff, and directed by Barnett R. Rubin. CPA operates under the guidance of a distinguished advisory board representing a wide range of disciplines and expertise (see Appendix F for a list of members). CPA has been funded by the Carnegie Corporation of New York, The Century Foundation (formerly the Twentieth Century Fund), the United States Institute of Peace, and the Winston Foundation.

Many of today's most serious international problems—ethnic conflicts, failing states, and humanitarian disasters—could be averted or ameliorated given effective early attention. CPA defines preventive action as those steps that can be taken in a volatile situation to prevent a crisis.

In order to study the prevention of such crises, CPA selected four case studies—the Great Lakes region of Central Africa, the Ferghana Valley region of Central Asia, Nigeria, and the South Balkans. For each case study, CPA assembled diverse and experienced practitioners and experts in working groups and sent a delegation on a study mission to map out strategies for settling or managing the conflict.

CPA draws on the knowledge gained from all four case studies, the experience of others, and previous studies to determine what strategies are most effective in the field of preventive action. In order to disseminate its recommendations for its case studies and its other findings, CPA has established, in collaboration with The Century Foundation (formerly the Twentieth Century Fund), a series of Preventive Action Reports. *Stabilizing Nigeria: Sanctions, Incentives, and Support for Civil Society* is the third volume in this series.

CPA PROJECT ON NIGERIA

Immediate tensions in Nigeria have arisen from the aborted democratic transition of June 1993 and the subsequent authoritarian course of General Sani Abacha's regime. Ethnic, religious, and regional tensions, as well as economic malaise, contribute to the potential for conflict. Due to Nigeria's dominant position in West Africa and its vast oil reserves, an eruption of conflict would have substantial regional and international repercussions. CPA's Nigeria project analyzes the interdependence of international public policy and Nigerian civil society in pressuring the military regime, preventing conflict, and assisting sustainable democratic reform.

After reviewing current international policy approaches toward Nigeria, CPA has outlined a strategy oriented toward longer-term aspects of governance and conflict resolution. This multifaceted approach combines pressure such as sanctions with support for civil society and conflict resolution mechanisms in the development of stable democratic politics in Nigeria.

CPA NIGERIA WORKING GROUP

The Nigeria Working Group is chaired by Professor Pearl T. Robinson and assisted by a consultant, Professor Peter M. Lewis. Its members represent a wide variety of fields and areas of expertise including religion, media, academia, business, human rights, and humanitarian work. (See Appendix B for a complete list of members.) The Working Group was assembled to provide guidance to the project, to review the report produced by the project, and to develop recommendations for policy in the region. Members of the Working Group met

several times in New York and Atlanta to map out strategies and proposals aimed at preventing instability and promoting sustainable democratic governance. In Atlanta members of the Working Group joined
the Carter Center's Nigeria Strategy Group for discussions. The relationship of both CPA's Working Group and the Carter Center's Strategy
Group to this report, however, is purely advisory, and the members of
these groups bear no responsibility for the views expressed here.

CPA STUDY MISSION TO NIGERIA

CPA sent some members of its Nigeria Working Group on a study
mission to Nigeria in January 1997. During the two-week trip the group
met with more than thirty organizations and numerous individuals in
four cities. The meetings were held in both southern and northern
locales, including groups from diverse ethnic, regional, and religious
communities. A broad range of interests were represented including
human rights groups, democracy activists, women's organizations, environmental groups, minority rights advocates, labor unions, academics,
the bar association, the media, conflict resolution groups, religious
denominations, the business community, politicians, retired military
officers, and spokesmen for government.

— EXECUTIVE SUMMARY —

For Africa and those concerned with it no country poses a greater challenge and a greater risk than Nigeria. It is Africa's most populous country, a major exporter of oil and potentially of natural gas, but its people's efforts to realize their potential have been frustrated by internal conflicts and misrule. The country was nearly torn apart by a secession movement and civil war from 1967 to 1970. Recent crises, set off by the annulment of the June 12, 1993, presidential election, once again raise the specter of internal conflict. Study of how to avert such an outcome has led the authors to the following conclusions:

- *The situation in Nigeria is urgent.* While significant economic interests and humanitarian values are at stake in Nigeria, the United States also has an important security interest: Nigeria shows signs of becoming a failed state with crumbling institutions and rising violence, which carries unpredictable consequences for its people, region, and continent. We note many indicators of conflict. Many countries display some of these indicators, but the presence of so many in Nigeria should be a warning of more trouble to come. They include:

  a) The continuing disaffection of key elites as a result of the annulment of the June 12, 1993, elections and the steps toward an uncontested presidential candidacy of the former military ruler, General Sani Abacha. The death of General Abacha on June 8, 1998, created an opportunity to resolve some of these tensions, and the successor government of General Abdulsalam Abubakar took some early steps toward reconciliation by releasing prominent political detainees. As this book went to press, however, we learned of the death in custody of Chief M. K. O. Abiola, presumed winner of the June 12, 1993, presidential elections. Abiola is reported to have died of a heart attack that occurred while he was speaking to a U.S. diplomatic delegation. Violence has broken out in Lagos and other southwestern cities, indicating the depth of the resentment and distrust in these areas. The government of General Abubakar will soon announce its plan for a democratic transition, but the death of Abiola will certainly make this task more difficult. More changes and unforeseen events are undoubtedly in the offing, some of which may make some of the recommendations in this report moot, for good or ill. Welcome as some of these developments may be, however, they should not be cause for complacency. Even if, despite the setback posed by Chief Abiola's untimely death, Nigeria starts the long march back from the precipice to which General Abacha's regime had taken it, much work is still required to establish legality, constitutionalism, accountability, and effective governance. Most of our analysis and recommendations bear on these longer-term issues, and we believe they still stand.

b) Increased signs of conflict within the military. The arrests in December 1997 of mainly Yoruba officers charged with yet another coup attempt seem to indicate that ethnic and regional resentment reaches into the army itself. The April 28, 1998, announcement of six death sentences for the alleged plotters after a closed trial led to violent demonstrations in Ibadan. The change of leadership in June 1998 also has the potential to incite further rivalries within the military. If these trends continue, the Nigerian military may no longer be able to provide the peacekeeping services in West Africa that have helped to legitimate it internationally in recent years.

c) A string of bombings and killings, some directed at the opposition and some at the government.

d) Political imprisonment and repression of free expression by the regime, despite a declared intention to undertake a transition to democracy. Despite the release of some detainees in June 1998, political freedoms are still constrained.

e) Repeated and seemingly increasing outbreaks of local violence in both the oil-producing Niger Delta and other regions of the country.

f) The growth and violent repression of grassroots Islamic move-ments in northern Nigeria.

g) The continuous economic decline despite Nigeria's oil wealth.

h) The decay of all of society's major institutions, including gov-ernment, the military, the judiciary, the civil service, educa-tion, transportation, and communication.

i) The continued growth of criminality and corruption.

j) The massive indifference or hostility to the Abacha government's official transition program shown by the vast majority of the popu-lation, as indicated in voter turnout for several rounds of elections.

- *Nigeria is entering a critical period.* The Abacha regime's electoral schedule called for polls in April and August, with a final hand-over date set for October 1, 1998. The manipulated nomination of Abacha for president by all five official political parties nullified the chance for even a limited transition. In the wake of Abacha's rule, there is clearly an opportunity to create a new framework for credible democratic reform. The choices of the military govern-ment and Nigeria's politicians will be critical for a stable, lasting transition. The rising stakes of political competition, the deep pop-ular misgivings about the credibility of the transition process, and the uncertain currents within the armed forces create a volatile situation. There are substantial possibilities for violence and insta-bility, comparable to the escalating unrest witnessed during the 1983 elections and in the run-up to the abortive transition of 1993. It is still necessary for the United States to take a strong position, together with international partners, to arrest these trends. An ambiguous stance will contribute to the type of large-scale con-flict we seek to avoid.

- *U.S. leadership is vital.* Such leadership has required, for some time, a strong and clear statement of policy from the president or secre-tary of state, followed by a vigorous, coordinated bilateral and mul-tilateral effort. That effort should include a clear and forceful statement of the problem and of what needs to be done, followed up by a multilevel communications strategy, a package of incen-tives if Nigeria becomes more inclusive and of sanctions if it fails to do so, and increased assistance to Nigerian civil society and prodemocracy groups that helps them link up across regional lines and connect Nigerians inside and outside the country.

- *The immediate goal of the U.S. effort should be to induce the Nigerian regime to undertake policies that remove the military from political rule, reverse political exclusion, and make debate, dialogue, and reconciliation possible.* This goal requires the following:

  a) A genuine military withdrawal from power. This should be a prominent feature of the United States' position. Inclusion and reconciliation can be assured only by an open, competitive process of transition to civilian rule. Candidates from the serving military, or civilians handpicked by the regime, should be adamantly discouraged. A viable transition must also be supported by a constitutional framework.

  b) The release of political detainees and prisoners. At this writing, there has been a hopeful development in the June 15 freeing of nine prominent detainees, including retired general Olusegun Obasanjo, human rights activist Beko Ransome-Kuti, and labor leaders Frank Kokori and Milton Dabibi. A number of human rights and prodemocracy advocates, journalists, and politicians remain in detention. The release of these remaining prisoners would be a major step toward opening the political system and fostering accord. There should also be an independent review of the sentences of many who have been convicted in unfair trials, including various accused coup plotters, and due process for those held pending trial, including a number of Ogoni detainees.

  c) An end to harassment of the media, in particular the closing of publications and detentions of and attacks on journalists.

  d) An end to harassment of dissident lawyers, politicians, social activists, and prodemocracy and human rights advocates; such measures have featured arbitrary detention, restrictions on freedom of movement, and physical attacks.

  e) The establishment of an independent electoral commission, such as monitored the annulled 1993 elections, for a new round of elections.

- *The United States should immediately begin high-level discussions with concerned nations and critical international organizations to reach a common position on these issues.* These include the United Kingdom, Canada, and South Africa, as well as the Commonwealth and the United Nations. Other major African states and the European Union should also be included. Since Abacha's program is no longer viable, the United States and international partners should seek a clear commitment from the Nigerian government to a new transition framework with a revised timetable. This transition should be supervised by a civilian-led, interim government, not the military, and should establish a legal and constitutional framework for the transition as a first prority. The international community should expect Nigeria's leadership to hold to the new schedule, and should specify incentives for adherence, or further sanctions if leaders do not respect the program. The United States government should build both domestic and international support for firm action.

- *If the Nigerian government continues on a course of military control and political exclusion, the United States should lead the international community in increasing the isolation of the Nigerian regime (not the country as a whole) through sanctions.* The best sanctions would be those targeted at the elites benefiting from the current arrangements, in particular those aimed at their assets abroad. As a second-best solution, if that proves too difficult, we should consider restrictions on additional international investment in the energy sector, on top of the existing restrictions on travel, military assistance, and access to international financial institutions. An embargo on payments for Nigerian oil exports should also be considered.

- *If the Nigerian government takes the necessary steps, the United States should lead the international community in preparing a series of incentives.* These should include debt relief, access to international financial institutions, new investments (especially outside the oil industry), support for restructuring civil-military relations, reconstruction of infrastructure, and support for privatization. These incentives, if implemented, form the essential elements of a long-term strategy.

- *Finally, whatever the actions of the Nigerian government, the United States and its partners should increase assistance to those Nigerians trying to build the base for a sustainable, multiethnic, federal democracy in their country.* This includes groups active in various sectors of civil society and prodemocracy groups. It should include both those in Nigeria and those abroad. Special attention should be paid to helping groups from neglected regions of the country, in particular the north; to linking up groups to those in other regions; and to linking up those inside the country with those outside. The democracy assistance funds that remain should be fully disbursed, and additional funds should be allocated.

• *In carrying out the democracy assistance, U.S. civil society and the private sector have vital roles.* Many private groups are active in Nigeria already and can expand their efforts as part of a broader strategy for encouraging change in that country:

a) NGOs, foundations, religious organizations, and others should expand existing links to Nigeria;

b) African-American organizations, women's organizations, and trade unions in particular should build on existing links and create new ones to anchor Nigerian civil society more firmly in international networks;

c) NGOs should either refuse to monitor noncompetitive elections or at least use any opportunities for election monitoring to conduct a full "democratic audit," examining freedoms of the press and association, political imprisonment, access to the party system, rule of law, and civil-military relations;

d) Foreign or international NGOs should sponsor meetings with Nigerian NGOs that would enable them to improve their coordination across region and sector;

e) U.S. religious organizations should take advantage of existing religious ties between the United States and Nigeria to strengthen Nigerian efforts at conflict resolution and reform;

f) U.S. Christian and Muslim groups in particular should strengthen engagement with their coreligionists in Nigeria;

g) Human rights and democracy-support organizations should make efforts to expand their ties with Nigerian organizations and assist Nigerians in forming better national and regional networks;

h) Conflict resolution organizations, universities, and think tanks should explore unofficial discussions among retired Nigerian and foreign military personnel and democratic activists to generate proposals for civil-military relations in a Nigerian democracy;

i) Businesses working in Nigeria should increase community development work through NGOs;

j) Businesses should support efforts by Nigerian businesses and NGOs to develop procedures for self-regulation and combating corruption;

k) Businesses should also support efforts by Nigerian business associations to improve economic governance.

Despite the many obstacles, Nigeria is not the hopeless case it is so often depicted as being. It has tremendous human and physical capital. The international community and the United States can enter into partnerships with Nigerians to assure that this capital is used in the interests of that country's people.

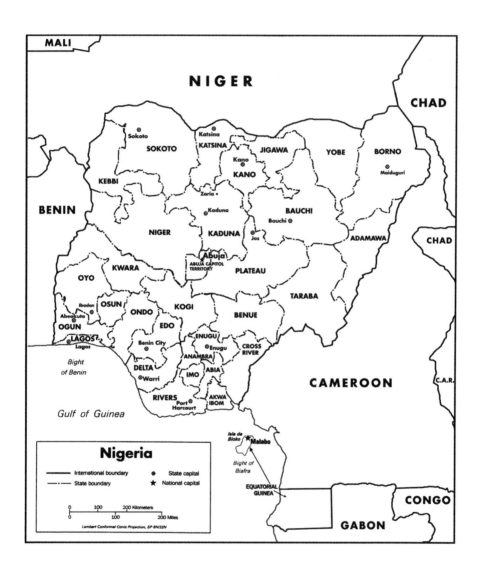

MALI

NIGER

CHAD

SOKOTO
Sokoto

KATSINA
Katsina

JIGAWA

YOBE

BORNO
Maiduguri

KEBBI

KANO
Kano

KANO

BENIN

Zaria

Kaduna

BAUCHI
Bauchi

NIGER

KADUNA

Jos

ADAMAWA

CHAD

KWARA

Abuja
ABUJA CAPITOL
TERRITORY

PLATEAU

OYO

TARABA

Ibadan
OSUN

Abeokuta

OGUN

LAGOS
Lagos

ONDO

KOGI

EDO

BENUE

ENUGU

Benin City

Enugu

CROSS
RIVER

DELTA

Warri

ANAMBRA

IMO

ABIA

Bight
of Benin

RIVERS

AKWA
IBOM

Port
Harcourt

CAMEROON

C.A.R.

Gulf of Guinea

Isla de
Bioko

Malabo

Bight of
Biafra

EQUATORIAL
GUINEA

CONGO

GABON

Nigeria

International boundary   ● State capital

State boundary   ★ National capital

0   100   200 Kilometers
0   100   200 Miles

Lambert Conformal Conic Projection, SP 8N/32N

— Part I —

Introduction

— 1 —

STATEMENT OF THE PROBLEM

"We need preventive diplomacy very much. Otherwise we are sleepwalking to disaster." These words from a prominent scholar at Bayero University of Kano in northern Nigeria surprised our group from the Council on Foreign Relations with their frankness and intensity. That this university official spent several hours with us in January 1997, as the hot afternoon lengthened during the fast days of the Muslim holy month of Ramadan, impressed us further with an appreciation of his commitment. A man long involved with the politics of his region and country, with close relations to both the highest officials of the current regime and those most opposed to them, he urged on us the need for international engagement with Nigeria. Its leaders, he argued, did not understand the dangers they were courting or the international reaction to their deeds.

For Africa and those concerned with it no country poses a greater challenge and a greater risk than Nigeria. It is Africa's most populous country, a major exporter of oil and potentially of natural gas, but its people's efforts to realize their potential have been frustrated by internal conflicts and misrule. The country was nearly torn apart by a secession movement and civil war during the period from 1967 to 1970. Recent crises, set off by the annulment of the June 12, 1993, presidential election, once again raise the specter of internal conflict.

To investigate the degree of danger and consider various strategies to meet it, the Council on Foreign Relations' Center for Preventive Action (CPA) held a series of meetings and consultations beginning in early 1996. CPA was formed by the Council in 1994 to study and test preventive action in international affairs. We consider the internal situation in Nigeria, as in other countries, a matter of legitimate international concern, not only because of international norms and humanitarian standards but also because a crisis in such a large and important country would inevitably have vast and unforeseeable international consequences. The United States continues to have important interests on the African continent, including growing economic stakes, concerns about instability that can have far-reaching disruptive effects, and growing ties between African-Americans and Africans. Nigeria is in many respects the key to sub-Saharan Africa: its continued decline would pull much of the continent down with it, while its revival would anchor positive trends in the region.

As a result of this process of planning and reflection, CPA sent a small study mission to Nigeria in January 1997.[1] The main focus of the mission was to learn about the views, activities, and capacities of Nigerian civil society, but it also tried to evaluate the potential for conflict and the prospects for better governance. The group traveled to Lagos, Ibadan, Kano, and Abuja over a period of two weeks.

During this brief visit, the group concluded that while a combination of repression and co-optation had succeeded in quelling the open mass protests of 1993 and 1994, the risk of violent conflict remained. Whereas international attention often focuses rightly on repression, the willingness of some of Nigeria's politicians to succumb to the Abacha regime's offers of jobs and favors was also an important factor. While some Nigerians we met expressed support for some policies pursued under military rule, none argued that it represented a legitimate or desirable system of government, and all deplored its effects. Most, however, also expressed deep skepticism of civilian politicians, who were often described as corrupt and prone to manipulating ethnic divisions. Since then, mass protest reemerged in response to General Abacha's steps to succeed himself as president and the death sentences passed on alleged coup plotters. It could erupt again should General Abacha's successors fail to meet hopes for a genuine transition.

Hence we conclude that concerted action is more necessary than ever to avert dangers of conflict. In the January mission we observed a number of warning signs, and since then troubling new developments have added others.

DANGERS

The warning signs include:

- The continuing disaffection of important segments of the population and key elites, a direct result of the retroactive annulment of the presidential election of June 12, 1993, which was apparently won by the business magnate Chief M. K. O. Abiola.[2] Abiola was jailed for treason a year later when he proclaimed himself president. This disaffection has been most pronounced among southerners, especially members of Abiola's Yoruba ethnic group but it exists throughout the country. The arrest on December 21, 1997, of mainly Yoruba military officers, including former military ruler General Sani Abacha's deputy, General Oladipo Diya, and one civilian on charges of plotting a coup d'état may indicate that such sentiments have even affected the military high command. The passage of death sentences on General Diya and five of his coaccused on April 28, 1998, inflamed demonstrations in Ibadan, where the police killed at least seven people. Similar ethnic conflicts within the military set the stage for the Biafran secession and civil war in 1967.

- Continued bombings and killings, some directed against government targets and some against opposition figures. These acts have included bombings aimed at military targets in several Nigerian cities, the unsolved assassination of Chief Abiola's wife, Kudirat, and several other attacks on prominent dissidents.[3]

- The persistence of military rule without popular representation, accompanied by selective political repression and intimidation, including regular harassment and jailing of journalists, even during a period of supposed transition to democracy. The unexplained death in prison of fifty-four-year-old former army chief of staff and political leader Shehu Yar'Adua on December 8, 1997, has raised alarm over what might happen to other detainees and prisoners.

- Repeated signs of dissent and conflict within the army itself. The Abacha government claimed it had uncovered several coup plots. In April 1995 it arrested, among others, former president Olusegun Obasanjo and Shehu Yar'Adua. Yar'Adua's original death sentence was commuted, but, as noted, he later died in prison under murky circumstances. The charges that eleven (mainly Yoruba) officers were planning a coup confirmed rumors that the military continued to be split at the highest levels. Despite conclusion of their military trial, public evidence has not fully substantiated the charges of coup plots, and the arrests and death sentences themselves prove the existence of severe tensions within the armed forces. The orderly succession of General Abdulsalam Abubakar following General Abacha's death is an encouraging sign, but there remain serious concerns about challenges from defiant or self-interested segments of the military.

- Repeated outbreaks of localized violence among ethnic and religious groups and growing opposition by local communities in the oil-producing southern delta regions to both the state and the oil companies, especially Royal Dutch/Shell. These conflicts came to international attention when the Nigerian government hanged on capital murder charges nine activists of the Ogoni ethnic group, including writer Ken Saro-Wiwa, during a meeting of the Commonwealth in November 1995. The disturbances have now expanded beyond the Ogoni to other communities in the Niger Delta. Toward the end of 1997, violence led to the closure of several pumping stations. In addition, local clashes leading to dozens of deaths have broken out in the western Ife region, which is not in the delta. Riots also erupted in majority Igbo towns in southeastern Nigeria in fall 1996. In early 1998 more violence erupted between nomads and farmers in both southwestern Oyo and northeastern Gombe states, killing as many as thirty-five people. Many other such incidents are not reported.

- The growth and violent repression in northern Nigeria of grassroots, militant Islamic movements, opposing both the government and the northern establishment. Several hundred of these movements' militants are in jail. They increasingly influence student politics at the universities; they have been involved in several violent incidents; and they are extending organizational networks into the vacuum left by the decay of public institutions. The government has responded by arresting activists and firing on demonstrators.

- Continued economic decline, punctuated by crises such as the persistent fuel shortage since spring 1997, despite Nigeria's status as Africa's leading oil producer. The government has regularly missed its payments under joint venture agreements in the oil sector, drastically reducing capacity utilization in this industry, a primary source of government revenue. Similarly a fertilizer shortage in the northern breadbasket region led many producers not to plant, raising the threat of food shortages in 1998. These problems reflect chronic mismanagement and government corruption and disarray.

- Decay and disintegration of basic infrastructure and leading public institutions, including transport and communications, schools and universities, everyday administration, the judiciary, and the financial system.

- Pervasive criminality and corruption, not least the involvement in international drug trafficking and financial scams.

Working with Nigerians to tackle these problems is vital to the future of Africa as well as instrumental in safeguarding international security and economic structures. Violent conflict in Nigeria would pose a security threat to West Africa and beyond, while a stable and respected Nigeria could help provide security and leadership for the whole continent, as suggested by past governments' record of leadership in the South African struggle and even the Abacha regime's leadership of an apparently successful peacekeeping operation in Liberia (although its efforts in Sierra Leone are less successful and more unilateral).[4] A Nigeria at peace with its own people and the rest of the world could do far more. The conflicts in the Niger Delta have already disrupted oil production; wider or more violent conflict would delay development of Nigeria's vast, untapped reserves of natural gas, which industry analysts describe as the "fuel of the twenty-first century." And the continued entrapment of Nigeria's 100 million people in a system where per capita income continues to fall despite $10 billion of annual oil income is both a human misfortune and a loss to the international economy.

The regime of General Abacha at one time announced policies ostensibly aimed at combating some of these problems. It claimed that its political transition program would lead to election of a civilian government by October 1, 1998, but this turned into a stage-managed process for Abacha to succeed himself as a superficially "civilianized" president, without any of the guarantees for human rights, free expression, political and legal control of the security forces, or political competition that actually constitute democracy. Economic reforms (assisted by a fortuitous rise in oil prices) tackled some of the mid-level corruption in financial institutions, reduced inflation, and pushed GDP growth above 3 percent in 1996. All of these accomplishments, unfortunately, were reversed by mid-1997 in the face of the fuel scarcity and questions over political clientelism in the government's handling of the "reformed" banks. Nonetheless, in January 1998 more failed banks were closed, a needed step toward restructuring. Meetings such as the yearly economic summit among business and economic leaders and the Vision 2010 conference have attempted to mobilize key elites around an agenda for economic reform and growth. Members of the CPA group attended several sessions of Vision 2010 and met with its president, former head of state Chief Ernest Shonekan. While those participating raised some of the issues critical to economic progress in Nigeria, the sessions did not address the fundamental question of governance. Their centerpiece was a presentation of the "Malaysian model," supposedly the Asian version of authoritarian capitalism. Since that meeting, of course, the Asian financial crash has exposed the liabilities in that model attributable to the lack of accountability and transparency. The economic experience of Nigeria under military regimes only reinforces that lesson. Though during our visit a number of Nigerians otherwise critical of the government gave it some credit for its economic policies, the fiascoes of 1997 largely nullified those efforts. In the context of political exclusion, mismanagement, and corruption, as well as the ever harder struggle for survival, most Nigerians remain cynical and indifferent toward such efforts. As yet, the central issues of state—the role of the military and high-level massive corruption—urgently require public debate.

DIAGNOSIS

While the immediate problems of military rule, human rights, and elections attract the most attention, Nigeria's problems reach back far before June 12, 1993. Except for a few months after the first military coup, all of Nigeria's constitutions have recognized that the country's ethnic composition requires federalism, and this now appears to form part of a national consensus. In our view functioning federalism in Nigeria will also need things no constitution can require, namely carefully negotiated power sharing and continual dialogue among ethnic and religious communities. Nigeria's economy, however, dependent on oil exports for 90 percent of foreign exchange and 80 percent of government revenues, enhances centralization because the $10 billion in revenues a year generated by oil go directly to the central powerholders. Many leaders have become rich through politically inspired partnerships in oil trading ventures, misuse or misallocation of funds, and diversion of revenues. Such corruption has undermined much of Nigeria's institutional framework, most especially the federal system. The easy availability of such funds also relieves the state of the need for taxation and enables a small group of rulers to undertake public spending and policy without accountability.

The country nearly split over economically charged ethnic issues in the 1960s, when a civil war in which perhaps two million died prevented the oil-rich eastern region from seceding as the independent state of Biafra. Since then a variety of attempts to handle Nigeria's diversity through federal and other schemes have foundered on the weakness of institutions. The state's increasing dependence on oil revenues combined with military authoritarianism makes control of the central government a winner-take-all proposition, raising fears of exclusion by all losers. Oil dependence facilitates central control by the military, feeds corruption, and has undermined institutional reform.

The structure of the economy fuels ethnic tensions. While Nigeria's diverse groups are involved in a complex system of competition and cooperation, at the national level there are three large regional-ethnic coalitions that predominate. These three groups—the Hausa-Fulani, Yoruba, and Igbo—are generally considered regionally predominant, while other groups are sometimes lumped together as "minorities."

The elites of northern Nigeria, many from the Hausa-speaking group, including the former Fulani aristocracy, have been politically dominant since independence. Access to the central state enables them to benefit from the flow of oil revenues, which do not originate in their region. Within the north, other groups, such as the Kanuri, who ruled much of the area before the Fulani conquest in the nineteenth century and to which General Abacha belonged, also play important roles. Between the northern zone and the south, properly speaking, is the highly diverse "middle belt," home to many small ethnic groups and the site of the new federal capital, Abuja. This area has been the scene of many local conflicts over land and other resources, which often take on religious or ethnic connotations.

Major private-sector commercial and financial resources are concentrated in Lagos, the former federal capital and still the commercial capital. Lagos is a multiethnic, cosmopolitan city in which all groups have some presence, but it is located in the predominantly Yoruba southwest. Hence, according to many Nigerians from both north and south, some northern elites perceived the election of Abiola, a Yoruba, as president to be an unacceptable concentration of political and financial power in one group. In any case, they feared loss of their privileged access to the state and its oil revenues. Some northerners likewise fear privatization that will move assets away from control of public institutions, within which they are entrenched; the private sector is dominated by southerners. Many Yorubas, on the other hand, have largely perceived these reactions as not only antidemocratic but also as evidence of an oligarchic monopoly of power and the exclusion of Yorubas from full citizenship in Nigeria.

Igbo political leadership based in eastern Nigeria has maneuvered for advantage between these two poles, often tilting toward the north. This partly reflects the legacy of the civil war, when the Yoruba leaders of western Nigeria disappointed the leaders of Biafra in the east by deciding to support the north in the suppression of the secessionist movement. The former eastern region also includes much of the Niger Delta, where most of Nigeria's onshore oil resources are located. The delta has been the scene of protest movements by ethnic groups, notably the Ogoni, who have paid the costs of oil development on their land without receiving benefits in the form of social services and political representation. As a result this area has become the scene of some of the most intense government repression.

Some political leaders from all groups, of course, have maintained stands based on principle, not ethnic affiliation, but since the nullification of June 12 and the subsequent manipulation of ethnicity to justify this act, this became more difficult. The collapse of Abacha's transition program, however, may push democratic forces to overcome these differences.

As a result of this history, typical political views differ among the regions, though each is also highly diverse internally. What they all share, however, is the traumatic experience of the 1967-70 civil war, which demonstrated the costs of division and helped to cement Nigeria as a federal state. While cynicism toward those in power, military or civilian, seems nearly universal, the sense of grievance since 1993 has been expressed much more intensely in the south. Those who actively oppose the government in the north may do so in Islamic rather than secular democratic terms. While Islamic and democratic movements are not necessarily antithetical, they are at least organizationally and ideologically distinct. And in the ethnically charged environment after the nullification, even secular northern prodemocracy activists did not ally with the partisans of June 12. In the east a lingering resentment that the Western Region allied with the north against Biafra during the civil war enabled some political leaders to justify siding with the government against a purportedly Yoruba June 12 cause. Minority groups may nurse particular grievances against their neighbors, the dominant group in their area, or the state, and these may be intensified by competition over control of local governments. In the absence of representative institutions to resolve conflict, the government has tended to try to contain ethnic demands by creating ever smaller federal units, a process that often leads to further conflicts over control of the patronage resources such local governments receive.

Religious groups also differ broadly in their political orientation, though, again, each is diverse. Mainstream Christian leaders have been relatively outspoken in condemning human rights violations and calling for a return to democracy, while those belonging to evangelical or syncretic sects have been more quietist. Some of these sects, however, indirectly reflect political realities by speaking of a "Gospel of Democracy." Official Muslim leaders are divided between those from the northern emirates and those from the Yoruba areas. In the northern emirate areas both the emirs and the shari'a court judges are paid by the state. They are a key part of the leadership of the northern elites. Yoruba Muslim leaders have no such quasi-official roles and were in some cases closely identified with Abiola's candidacy. The Islamic establishment in the north also faces growing populist challenges within its own society.

The inability to settle these basic structural issues among the regions and ethnic groups created a vacuum into which the military has stepped, not unwillingly. It has continued to manipulate them to justify its rule. Access to power, and hence oil money, has also enabled Nigeria's military rulers and their supporters to enrich themselves. After the ethnic-based coups that led to the Biafran war, ethnic relations in the military seem to have received close attention. Even before the December 1997 arrests of mainly Yoruba military officers, forced retirements had reduced the ethnic diversity of the officer corps, in particular by reducing the number of southerners, and key positions of internal control (notably the chief of staff, a position central to coup making) have been largely held by northerners. The rule of Abacha's military predecessor, Ibrahim Babangida, a middle-belt Muslim, was resented by some northern elites. These elites, allied with northern army officers (Abacha, formerly Babangida's chief of staff, was a Kanuri from Kano), reportedly worked to encourage the annulment of the June 12, 1993, election.[5]

These long-term structural problems underlie the immediate problems of military rule, corrupt governance, and political exclusion. The immediate causes, however, were the annulment of the 1993 elections and the palace coup of General Abacha in November 1993. On October 1, 1995, Abacha announced a new transition supposedly to democratic rule, set to conclude by October 1, 1998. Abacha effectively nullified the transition by arranging for all official parties to nominate him to succeed himself. Furthermore, the new constitution under which the transition was to take place was never made public, so that no one knew the powers of the president. This new constitution also reportedly called for rotation of the presidency and other offices among six newly defined geocultural zones, an awkward system that seems even to surpass the old Yugoslavia in its potential for deadlock and entrenched conflict.

In the course of Abacha's transition program, some observers held a slim hope that the general would refrain from succeeding himself and allow for the replacement of military rule by an elected civilian government. In the final months of Abacha's rule, even this hope was dashed.The inherent flaws in the transition removed the possibility that it could serve as a vehicle for political liberalization. The transition plan did not include an institutional commitment by the military to withdraw from power, nor was it democratic in even a minimal sense. The stringent requirements for political party registration (five groups were handpicked from more than thirty applications) effectively eliminated genuine opposition groups and important leaders from contention; imprisonment silenced the apparent winner of the previous election as well as other leaders; continuing intimidation and repression of media prevented open discussion; and lack of an independent electoral commission undermined faith in the process.[6] General Abacha's steps to succeed himself were the coup de grace to an already discredited process.

The government did not undertake any process of negotiation or reconciliation with the supporters of June 12. The apparent victor of that election remained in detention. In his independence day speech on October 1, 1997, General Abacha's appeal to the aggrieved was limited to asking them to participate in elections from which they had been excluded a priori. Nor was there any public discussion of civil-military relations. Critical articles about military institutions or intramilitary politics regularly led to the detention of journalists. The new military authorities have an opportunity to address these basic problems. Until all political prisoners are released and uninhibited public discussion is permitted, however, dialogue and reconciliation cannot move forward.

Whatever chances of success such eventual dialogue or reconciliation may have will be proportionate to the strength of civil society in Nigeria. Especially in view of the disarray of the political class, civil society is likely to play a key role in any genuine transition. Human rights organizations, Christian and Muslim associations, women's groups, grassroots health projects, universities, trade unions, business associations, media outlets, conflict resolution institutes, think tanks, and others provide the indispensable underpinnings for a more plural and accountable state and economy. At present some of these organizations suffer from selective repression, and they are fragmented for various reasons, despite some attempts to combine efforts. Their potential capacities and skills are impressive, however. Rather than look primarily abroad for training and organizational assistance, as do fledgling NGOs in some countries, Nigerians are providing it themselves. Some new NGO sectors still rely a great deal on international funding, while established elements of civil society (religion, press, trade unions) do not. All, however, confront both repression and the ethnic, regional, and religious fragmentation of the country. Their members repeatedly told our group that they are less in need of direct external assistance than of pressure on the government to release prisoners and let them work freely. Many would also welcome support for their efforts at creating networks and alliances across sectors, regions, ethnicities, and religions both domestically and internationally.

— 2 —

RECOMMENDATIONS

Policy toward Nigeria must address both the short- and long-term issues, and must be carried out by both official organizations (governments and international institutions) and private ones (civil society). The goal of policy should be to develop firm partnerships with Nigerians to work for a country that is governed through legitimate, effectively functioning institutions and that uses its hydrocarbon wealth to invest in diversified development for the benefit of its people. To achieve these goals, we recommend that the U.S. government and the international community apply pressures and offer significant incentives, both linked to clear benchmarks; undertake a coordinated effort at coherent communication with the Nigerian authorities, elites, and diverse public audiences; and that international organizations, especially unofficial ones, engage even more actively with Nigerian civil society and democratic groups.

In the short run, even if it proves impossible to go back to the political compact of June 12, the wounds it has caused cannot be wished away. By allowing Abacha to declare his intention to run unopposed with minimal international opposition, the international community failed to do what it could to assure that the regime honored its own promises for a transition. The shift of military leadership in June 1998 creates new possibilities for change. International actors must demand the withdrawal of the military from power, the release of political prisoners, establishment of the conditions for open dialogue and debate, and a program of genuinely free and fair elections. Only open discussion, free of threats and fear, can mitigate the divisions caused by the annulment of the election, ease future civil-military relations, and address the deeper concerns on all sides of the regional divides.

Failure of the Nigerian authorities to meet these conditions should provoke a strong, negative international response, including imposition of economic sanctions. Meeting them should prompt an equally strong, positive international response. In return for the needed political opening, the international community should offer Nigeria a package of economic support, which might include debt relief, aid in reconstructing its infrastructure and managing its oil revenues, and access to capital and export markets. The specific package would, of course, depend on direct consultations at the time. Regardless of the Nigerian government's course of action, both governments and private organizations should, to the extent possible, work with the Nigerian democratic opposition and civil society to develop international partnerships and assist them with the needs they identify.

The international community must recognize that the Nigerian public's attitudes are diverse, and this includes their attitudes toward foreign participation. While Western criticism of the Nigerian government is often welcomed in the south, some in the north see it as anti-Nigerian or anti-Muslim, as it is so portrayed by the government and allied elites. Although Abiola is a Muslim with many family and business connections in the north, some there, and not only Abacha's direct beneficiaries, have attributed Western sympathies for June 12 to the greater international connections of the Yorubas. These feelings have been strengthened by a campaign of defamation against Yorubas that seemed to enjoy the support of some in the establishment. In Kano our group received copies of an obviously forged pamphlet, "The Yoruba Agenda," claiming to reveal a vast Yoruba plot to capture control of the country. Hence it is no less important for foreigners concerned with Nigeria than for Nigerians themselves to recognize this diversity. While maintaining and strengthening links to the better-known groups in the south, we should also make special efforts to reach groups elsewhere, particularly predominantly Muslim groups in the north.

Our more specific recommendations are:

PRESSURES

- The United States, United Kingdom, Canada, the Commonwealth, and the European Union should maintain at least the current level of targeted sanctions (travel and visa restrictions, no military aid) until: (1) a transition to civilian rule takes place, (2) political prisoners are released, and (3) barriers to free public discussion and debate are removed. Conditions for intensifying sanctions are discussed below. We emphasize that all three of these conditions are necessary. Those who should be released include, but are not limited to, Chief Abiola, the Ogoni detainees, and all labor leaders, journalists, and human rights activists. Regrettably, it is no longer possible to release General Yar'Adua. Death sentences passed on the alleged coup plotters arrested in December 1997 should be commuted, and all cases should be reviewed by independent tribunals. While these prisoners have different legal statuses—some detained without charge, some pending trial, and some serving court-imposed sentences—the shadow over the judicial process during military rule has been such that we believe all must be released or have an independent review of their trials for the sake of a new start.

- Clear benchmarks for the easing or intensification of these international sanctions should be established. It must be made known that current sanctions will remain until political prisoners are released and a transition to civilian rule takes place, and sanctions will be intensified if the government does not hand over power, release political prisoners, and permit unfettered debate in a timely fashion. The intensified sanctions should focus on financial measures against the regime and individuals who profit from it, including a ban on transactions by the regime and its key figures. These accounts are reported to be mainly in the Middle East and Europe, and the intelligence, diplomatic, and legal work necessary to freeze these assets should begin immediately. Such preparations could include formation of an international working group representing the Commonwealth and major purchasers of Nigerian oil. It is important to build the international coalition needed to make these sanctions effective. Growing public support for such sanctions in the United States through grassroots movements and legislation will also make them more feasible.

- International corporations working in Nigeria should convey to the Nigerian authorities the need to release political prisoners and implement a transition to civilian rule in order to maintain normal commercial relations, which are inevitably endangered by the instability that Nigeria now risks. They should also frankly inform the government of the political risks posed by the grassroots movement for sanctions against Nigeria and companies working there, which will inevitably grow if the military fails to leave power.

- The U.S. government and its international partners should initiate proactive consultations on Nigeria with major oil companies operating there to prepare them for sanctions and minimize political friction based on commercial competition among different companies and states.

INCENTIVES

- Governments, international financial institutions, and corporations should present to the Nigerian authorities and public a comprehensive plan of economic incentives that will be available once Nigeria is clearly embarked on the path of civilian rule, inclusion, and dialogue. While any specific agenda will have to develop out of dialogue and evaluation of needs at that time, these could include:

  a) Substantial relief and restructuring of Nigeria's external debt, which would of course also have to be linked to implementation of an appropriate economic policy framework and accountability and transparency of expenditures;

  b) Aid for creating accountable institutions for the handling of oil revenues, including democratically monitored special allotments for communities adversely affected by oil production;

  c) Access to export markets;

  d) Support for a privatization and stabilization program that does not unduly burden the Nigerian public or intensify ethnic competition;

  e) Assistance and investment in reconstruction of transportation, power, and communications facilities;

  f) Support for major investments beyond the energy sector, with special incentives for investment in neglected regions.

- During the interim period, in order to hold out more effective incentives, the Commerce Department could assemble a group of corporations interested in investing in Nigeria that are currently deterred by the prospect of instability and corruption. Whether through a high-level corporate visit or other means, the U.S. government could make it known to the Nigerian government and public how much potential investment they are losing as a result of the political environment.

CLEAR COMMUNICATION

- Since June 1993 there has been no clear, high-level statement of U.S. policy toward Nigeria. Instead, the United States has tried many ways to communicate its concerns to the Nigerian government, including direct discussions by the embassy, led by Ambassador Walter Carrington and his recent successor, Ambassador William Twaddell, confidential discussions in Geneva, and the sending of special envoys such as Ambassadors Donald McHenry and Bill Richardson (then a member of the House of Representatives). Shortly before the death of General Abacha, the Nigerian authorities rejected a U.S. proposal to send a senior delegation led by Under Secretary of State Thomas Pickering. CPA's working group on Nigeria heard about the difficulty of communicating with the authorities in Nigeria from many, including American diplomats and corporations. Shortly after Abacha's death, both the president and the secretary of state made statements urging the Nigerian government to release political prisoners and to open a competitive process of transition to civilian rule. These statements should be reiterated, and senior officials should carefully evaluate the course taken by Nigeria's new military ruler. An unambiguous, high-level statement of policy can provide the context to make all other communications more effective. In such a context, efforts by the U.S. government to communicate its policy clearly to the Nigerian regime, elites, and people should immediately be increased. Just as the Nigerian government has expended funds and hired public relations firms to promote its views among key constituencies in this country, the United States should not only increase communication with those in power but also seek to reach other constituencies in Nigeria. Such engagement is complementary, not contradictory, to the use of pressure and incentives.

- Discussions with the Nigerian authorities should include other topics of concern (such as drug trafficking and West African security), with the understanding that cooperation on these issues will be helpful, but care should be taken not to give the impression that cooperation on these issues can substitute for domestic political initiatives. The United States should also actively support and promote the emerging African consensus that security includes democratization and the development of norms and sanctions against coups d'état and military regimes.

- In the context of such a strategy, the United States could consider using its military officers to communicate with the military regime and, once a transition is in place, to provide assistance in defining an appropriate framework for civil-military relations; military assistance, sales, and training should resume only when such a framework is firmly in place. Any delegation dealing with military affairs should include and be led by civilian experts in military affairs, in order to reinforce the message of civilian control of the military.

ENGAGEMENT WITH CIVIL SOCIETY

- The U.S. government, the European Union, and others should immediately increase support to Nigerian civil society and democratic groups.

- Foundations, nongovernmental organizations, religious organizations, and others should take an inventory of existing links to Nigeria in order to plan how to expand their work. Noting that many such efforts are already under way, we also suggest consideration of the following:

  a) NGOs should not agree to monitor patently undemocratic elections. Instead, they could use opportunities to visit the country to conduct a full "democratic audit" (a concept developed by the democratic movement of Kenya), examining freedoms of the press and association, political imprisonment, access to the party system, rule of law, and civil-military relations. If an unambiguous process of free and fair elections were to be launched—a process meeting the benchmarks we have outlined above—there might be a role for more conventional electoral assistance by NGOs.

b) Perhaps taking advantage of institutions in other African countries, foreign or international NGOs should sponsor meetings
with Nigerian NGOs and opposition groups that would enable
them to improve their linkage and coordination across region
and sector. Any such meetings should attempt to bring a representative regional and religious mix of Nigerians to the table.
The International Human Rights Law Group held such a meeting in Ghana in June 1998.

c) Religious organizations should examine how they can make use
of the numerous religious ties between the United States and
Nigeria to strengthen Nigerian efforts at conflict resolution and
reform; given the particular importance of Christian-Muslim
relations in Nigeria, American Christians and Muslims should
examine how to strengthen engagement with their coreligionists in Nigeria; one proposal has been to collaborate with
Christian-Muslim ecumenical organizations in other African
countries, notably South Africa, to sponsor broad Christian-
Muslim discussion on the future of Nigeria.

d) Human rights and democracy support organizations should
make special efforts to expand their existing ties with Lagos-
based organizations, to extend them to counterparts in other
regions, and to assist Nigerians in forming better national and
regional networks. Attempts by these organizations to ally
with other sectors of civil society should be supported.

e) Conflict resolution organizations, universities, or think tanks
should explore unofficial discussions among democratic activists
and retired Nigerian and foreign military figures to generate
proposals for reforming civil-military relations in a Nigerian
democracy. Nigeria has a long history of discussion of these
issues, which needs to be revived and updated as it cannot be in
a repressive environment.

f) Businesses working in Nigeria should increase community
development work through NGOs and include development
of local representative and civil society institutions as part of
community development; they should also support efforts
by Nigerian business and by NGOs such as Transparency
International to develop procedures for self-regulation and

combating corruption; international corporations could also support efforts by Nigerian business associations to improve economic governance.

g) African-American organizations, women's organizations, trade unions, and many others should build on existing links and create new ones to attach Nigerian civil society more firmly to international counterparts.

There are, of course, a number of existing efforts by U.S.-based private groups to engage with Nigerian civil society concerning political issues. Corporations have supported efforts to improve the climate for investment, as through the economic summit and the Vision 2010 process. A broad coalition of human rights and Nigerian exile groups has supported a movement for sanctions against both the Nigerian government itself and corporations doing business in Nigeria. The movement has led to sanctions against companies by some U.S. local governments and the introduction of legislation in Congress.

We see some potential benefit in both efforts. Engagement with Nigerians in pursuit of economic reform will be essential to the strategy we have outlined here. While the Abacha regime was clearly incapable of implementing the needed reforms, the direction of his successors has yet to be fully defined. Corporations that are serious about helping Nigerians create a positive environment for investment, growth, and development will have to take some political risks and speak the truth about the need for political change as a necessary condition for economic transformation. At the least they should not actively resist policies of their own governments aimed at supporting democratic change.

The sanctions movement should be a wake-up call for anyone in the Nigerian leadership who thinks that international opposition to violations of human rights, corruption, and military rule is temporary or the result of misunderstandings or plots. The same organizations, in many cases, worked for decades against apartheid in South Africa. They are now taking up the cause of democracy in Nigeria, and they are steadily expanding the base of support for their effort. They are doing so in collaboration with some of those Nigerians most firmly opposed to military rule, providing them with an external source of moral support despite the hardships they face at home.

The specific measures recommended here may diverge in part from some of those proposed by that movement, but we think all of us agree on one big point: the United States and the international community have a responsibility and an interest to undertake firm action to reverse the course of decline and repression down which Nigeria has been careening. The government of Nigeria can end the sanctions movement by ending military rule, releasing prisoners, permitting free public discussion, and holding genuine elections. If it does so, businesses, international financial institutions, and others will be able to make much more effective efforts to support the economic reforms that are so badly needed.

But if we have learned any lesson from the work of the Center for Preventive Action over the past few years, it is that these efforts by the private sector and nongovernmental organizations, while they are necessary, will not work without the leadership of committed states, most particularly the United States. NGOs and the private sector can undertake actions that governments cannot, but unless real power and resources are placed in the balance, the private efforts will not have the framework they need for success. There are constituencies that can be mobilized to support a more active U.S. policy on Nigeria, but despite a lengthy "policy review," the policy appears to have been low-key and reactive, partly as a result of international reliance on the Nigerian military as peacekeepers in Liberia and Sierra Leone.

This, then, is the classic problem of prevention. Hotter crises monopolize foreign policy. Perhaps Nigeria, despite repression, mismanagement, decay, ethnic and religious enmities, and endemic, low-level violence, will be able to muddle through without disturbing the rest of the international community too much. Perhaps action can be postponed. Perhaps it will be something for the next administration to worry about.

If, however, the U.S. administration is serious about its new focus on Africa and the reasons it gives that Americans should be concerned about Africa, postponing action on Nigeria is shortsighted and even self-defeating. If Nigeria erupts in a major conflict, there will be no economic and political revival in West Africa, and perhaps none further beyond. With a certain degree of hesitation occasioned by differences of opinion, the Commonwealth has kept Nigeria on the agenda and continued to focus on it. But at this historical juncture, it is only the United States that can formulate a strategy and lead a coalition to confront one of the world's most difficult problems. The United States did it, though too late, in the former Yugoslavia. It is imperative for Washington to lead such a coalition to prevent what could be an even greater disaster. America should do so bearing in mind that Nigeria, despite all that has befallen it, still has the potential to be a great success.

— PART II —

SUPPORTING MATERIAL

— 3 —

HISTORICAL BACKGROUND

In this section we provide some perspective on Nigeria's contemporary problems, reviewing the milestones and trends that have shaped the country's development in recent decades. The overview includes the colonial origins of the contemporary Nigerian state, the central alignments and institutions that have inspired political competition since independence, and the social and economic sources of instability. While offering a survey of historical developments, we focus mainly on the events of the past several years.

With a population estimated at 110 million, Nigeria is Africa's most populous country. It is also among the region's most diverse societies, encompassing some 250 ethnic and linguistic groups and numerous religious communities. The nation is somewhat less than half Muslim and about 45 percent Christian, with a wide array of affiliations within these broad traditions. Economically, Nigeria has a major presence on the African continent. It has the largest economy in West Africa, producing 80 percent of the total output within the sixteen-member Economic Community of West African States (ECOWAS). Since the late colonial era, the country's size and social makeup have posed challenges to stable governance and equitable development. In the decades since independence, these problems have been aggravated by the dramatic changes emanating from the petroleum economy.

The core themes of Nigerian history are contained in the challenges of stability, democracy, and development. Contentious ethnic divisions and precarious civil-military relations have made for recurrent political uncertainty. These factors have posed formidable hazards for the establishment of lasting democratic rule, which has been a perennial goal of most Nigerian leaders and citizens. The difficulties of sustaining growth and popular welfare amid a volatile export economy have mingled with the challenges of social equity and political change.

COLONIAL BEGINNINGS: 1914–60

The boundaries of present-day Nigeria contain a great variety of historical political units, social orders, cultures, and economic arrangements. The northern savanna was dominated by the Sokoto Caliphate, established by the jihad of Usman dan Fodio from 1804 to 1808. The Fulani leadership of Sokoto presided over a multiethnic Muslim empire, incorporating the Hausa states along with several minorities including Nupe, Gwari, and Yoruba. It was flanked to the east by the old Kanuri empire of Borno. The coastal and forest regions west of the Niger River were home to Yoruba and Edo states as well as other groups, while the areas to the east included several small states and segmentary lineage societies, of which the Igbo were the largest.

European involvement in Nigeria began with Portuguese contact in the late fifteenth century, but it was not until 1861 that Britain established the coastal Colony of Lagos, followed in 1900 by the Protectorates of Southern and Northern Nigeria. These units were amalgamated in 1914 to form a single colonial entity. The British maintained separate administration over the northern and southern zones, though. The application in Northern Nigeria of Sir Frederick Lugard's doctrine of indirect rule provided for considerable insulation of local political and religious institutions. In 1939, the colonial government created three regions with separate ethnic composition and economic patterns.

The Northern, Eastern, and Western regions each incorporated a single dominant ethnic group and numerous regional minorities.[1] Together, these major ethno-linguistic groups—the Hausa-Fulani, Igbo, and Yoruba—comprised two-thirds of Nigeria's people, a pattern that has had lingering effects on the course of political development. The predominantly Muslim Northern Region encompassed the nineteenth-century Hausa-Fulani emirates as well as the historical empire of Borno; the region also included Kanuri, Nupe, Kabe, and Tiv populations. The Western Region, where the Yoruba were the preeminent group, contained Edo, Ijaw, Urhobo, Igbo, and additional minorities. The Igbo were the largest group in the Eastern Region, which included Efik, Ibibio, and other groups. The capital, Lagos, was a traditionally Yoruba city in the southwestern corner of the country. These cultural and lin-guistic variations were paralleled by distinct export activities centered on cocoa in the west, palm oil in the east, and cotton and groundnuts in the north.

A rapid growth of anticolonial activism after World War II led to a negotiated settlement between Nigerian nationalists and the British government, heralding a period of gradual transition to independence in 1960. A series of political reforms culminated with the 1951 consti-tution, which established the outlines of a federal government. The creation of elected regional and federal assemblies gave substantial political leverage to ethnically based parties in the separate regions. A 1954 constitutional revision provided the regional governments with broader legislative and fiscal powers. The regions were each controlled by their leading political party, and the party that carried a plurality in the national legislature would form the federal government.

During the 1950s three major parties consolidated their regional bases of control, and their leaders attained both local power and nation-al prominence.[2] Nnamdi Azikiwe, head of the Igbo-dominated National Council of Nigeria and the Cameroons (NCNC—later renamed the National Convention of Nigerian Citizens) became premier of the Eastern Region. Obafemi Awolowo of the Yoruba-based Action Group (AG) ascended to the Western Region premiership, and Alhaji Ahmadu Bello, who held the traditional title of Sardauna of Sokoto, led the Northern Region government by virtue of his leadership of the Northern People's Congress (NPC), chiefly based among the Hausa-Fulani.

Throughout the late colonial period and the years of the First Republic, these parties sought to fend off opposition from regional minorities and contending national political forces. By the date of inde-pendence, the regions were governed under virtual single-party rule. Even in the Northern Region, where the conservative NPC faced a spirited challenge from the populist Northern Elements Progressive Union (NEPU) under Aminu Kano, the dominance of the ruling elite was unshaken. At the federal level, political competition was defined by the contention among leading regional parties. This was essentially a three-way struggle, although minority interests gained increasing polit-ical leverage throughout the period.

The terms of transfer from colonial rule yielded northern domi-nance of the first postindependence government. The 1957 constitu-tional settlement, which the British negotiated with Nigerian nationalists, allotted representation in the federal legislature on the basis of regional population. The 1952 colonial census indicated that the Northern Region included 53 percent of the total population. The NPC's decisive hold on the Northern Region ensured a plurality in the National Assembly, and Sir Abubakar Tafawa Balewa, deputy leader of the NPC, became prime minister in the new national administration. This arrangement was ratified in the 1959 transitional elections, in which the NPC maintained its position, and the British governor invited Tafawa Balewa to form the government. With control of the federal executive and a secure regional base, the leading northern party was in a uniquely advantageous position in federal politics. The northern elite was able to maintain control of the political center through selective alliance with, and exclusion of, rival southern parties.

THE FIRST REPUBLIC: 1960–66

The First Republic, commencing in October 1960, inherited the Westminster model of parliamentary rule and the three-region federal structure. Most observers agree that these institutions were fatal to the stability of the new democracy.[3] A constitutional republic was created in 1963. In a step toward ethnic balance, Dr. Azikiwe of the Eastern Region was named president. This reform had little effect on the competitive dynamics of the system. The dominance of the northern Hausa-Fulani elite in the federal government incited fears of political exclusion among other major ethno-regional groups. These concerns fostered extensive gerrymandering, electoral fraud, and political violence as ethnically centered parties attempted to preserve regional control and challenge northern dominance at the federal level. A zero-sum political struggle quickly eroded the stability and legitimacy of the regime.

The early years of the First Republic witnessed a complex series of battles over political formulas and alliances (see Table 3.1). The northern NPC entered into a coalition with the mainly eastern NCNC, marginalizing the Action Group in the west. When the AG was rent by factionalism shortly after independence, the dominant alliance seized upon the opportunity to weaken the party's influence. The federal authorities cast their support behind Chief S. L. Akintola, the Western Region premier, who was Chief Awolowo's leading rival. A state of emergency was imposed in the west, and the legislature voted to create a separate Midwestern Region. The new region was quickly captured by the NCNC. The partition of the Western Region undermined Awolowo's power and provided Akintola's new party, the Nigerian National Democratic Party (NNDP), with the opportunity to secure electoral control.

TABLE 3.1
MAJOR NIGERIAN POLITICAL PARTIES AND ORGANIZATIONS: 1960–PRESENT

Acronym	Name	Leader	Description
		FIRST REPUBLIC:	
NCNC	National Council of Nigeria and the Cameroons (later National Convention of Nigerian Citizens)	Nnamdi Azikiwe	Eastern Region/Igbo-dominated political party
AG	Action Group	Obafemi Awolowo	Western Region/Yoruba-dominated political party
NPC	Northern People's Congress	Ahmadu Bello	Northern Region/Hausa-Fulani-dominated political party
NEPU	Northern Elements Progressive Union	Aminu Kano	Northern, populist political party, represented challenge to NPC
UPGA	United Progressive Grand Alliance	—	Alliance of eastern NCNC, western AG, and northern NEPU
NNDP	Nigerian National Democratic Party	S. L. Akintola	Yoruba-based challenger to AG in Western Region
NNA	Nigerian National Alliance	—	Alliance of northern NPC and NNDP
		SECOND REPUBLIC:	
UPN	Unity Party of Nigeria	Obafemi Awolowo	Western/Yoruba political party (similar to old AG)
NPP	Nigerian People's Party	Nnamdi Azikiwe	Eastern/Igbo political party (similar to old NCNC)
PRP	People's Redemption Party	Aminu Kano	Northern, populist political party (similar to old NEPU)
GNPP	Great Nigerian People's Party	Waziri Ibrahim	Northeastern, breakaway political party from NPP
NPN	National Party of Nigeria	Shehu Shagari	Northern, centrist political party (similar to old NPC)
NAP	Nigerian Advance Party	Tunji Braithwaite	Independent, radical political party

TABLE 3.1 CONT.
MAJOR NIGERIAN POLITICAL PARTIES AND ORGANIZATIONS: 1960–PRESENT

Acronym	Name	Leader	Description
	ELECTIONS OF JUNE 12, 1993, AND AFTER:		
SDP	Social Democratic Party	M. K. O. Abiola	Center-left political party, established by government
NRC	National Republican Convention	Bashir Tofa	Center-right political party, established by government
ABN	Association for a Better Nigeria	Arthur Nzeribe	Movement in favor of President Babangida
ING	Interim National Government	Ernest Shonekan	Appointed by Babangida as national government, August 1993
NADECO	National Democratic Coalition	—	Pro-Abiola movement, launched May 1994
MOSOP	Movement for the Survival of the Ogoni People	—	Movement for Ogoni rights and environmental redress; included leader Ken Saro-Wiwa
	PARTIES OF THE ABACHA REGIME'S TRANSITION, OCTOBER 1996–?:		
UNCP	United Nigerian Congress Party	Alhaji Isa Mohammed, chair	Leading party in 1997 local government, state, and national assembly elections; officially approved party
DPN	Democratic Party of Nigeria	Alhaji Sule Ahmed, chair	Officially approved party
CNC	Congress for National Consensus	Alhaji Abel Ubeku, chair	Officially approved party
NCPN	National Center Party of Nigeria	Alhaji Magaji Abdullahi, chair	Officially approved party
GDM	Grassroots Democratic Movement	Alhaji Gambo Lawan, chair	Officially approved party

Sources: Richard Sklar, *Nigerian Political Parties* (Princeton, N.J.: Princeton University Press, 1964); Billy Dudley, *An Introduction to Nigerian Government and Politics* (Bloomington, Ind.: Indiana University Press, 1982); Larry Diamond, "Nigeria: The Uncivic Society and the Descent into Praetorianism," in Larry Diamond, Juan J. Linz, and Seymour Martin Lipset, eds., *Politics in Developing Countries,* 2d ed. (Boulder, Colo.: Lynne Rienner Publishers, 1996); Human Rights Watch/Africa, "Nigeria: Transition or Travesty? Nigeria's Endless Process of Return to Civilian Rule," *Human Rights Watch* 9, no. 6, (October 1977): 10.

These struggles were accompanied by controversy over the 1962 national census, inciting further competition for regional advantage. Initial figures showed large population increases in the south, but the NPC government challenged the results and pushed through a highly controversial recount, which restored the northern majority. The final tabulation in 1963 registered a large and scarcely credible increase in national population, suggesting a vigorous inflation of the tally by all regions. Elements of the NCNC were so angered by the census controversy that they withdrew from their coalition with the northern party.

The federal elections of 1964 served as a catalyst for stress throughout the political system. A shift in political alignments created further polarization in the electoral process. Having broken with northern conservatives, the eastern-based NCNC aligned with AG stalwarts from the west and the populist northern NEPU in a coalition dubbed the United Progressive Grand Alliance (UPGA). They were opposed by the Nigerian National Alliance (NNA), whose principal members were the northern, conservative NPC and Chief Akintola's western NNDP. A growing tide of violence, intimidation, and campaign infractions provoked an electoral boycott among disgruntled southern opposition parties. The NPC claimed a landslide in the Northern Region polls and achieved a free hand in forming a new federal government.

After an interlude of tense negotiations between Prime Minister Balewa and President Azikiwe the NPC coalition was able to take office while rescheduling elections for the regions affected by the boycott. Akintola's pro-NPC party won the Western Region elections in October 1965 through blatant vote rigging and suppression of the opposition. Mass violence in the aftermath of the elections led the NPC government to call on the military to sustain order. The government's evident weakness, in combination with mounting ethnic and regional tensions, prompted a military coup in January 1966. Nigeria's first attempt at democracy fell a casualty to sectional competition, political malfeasance, and military intrusion.

MILITARY RULE AND CIVIL WAR: 1966–70

The fissures within the Nigerian federation reached a crisis in 1966–67. The January coup was a violent revolt in which the prime minister, the Northern Region premier, and Chief Akintola were killed (see Table 3.2, page 34). The new military regime, dominated by eastern Igbo officers

TABLE 3.2
NIGERIAN HEADS OF STATE, 1960–PRESENT

NAME	DATES CIVILIAN	MILITARY/ ORIGIN	REGION OF	METHOD OF POWER TRANSFER
Abubakar Tafawa Balewa	Oct. 1960– Jan. 1966	Civilian	North	Killed in military coup
General Aguiyi Ironsi	Jan.–Jul. 1966	Military	East	Killed in military coup
Lt. Colonel (later General) Yakubu Gowon	Jul. 1966– Jul. 1975	Military	North (middle belt)	Deposed by military coup
Brigadier General Murtala Mohammed	Jul. 1975– Feb. 1976	Military	North	Killed in unsuccessful military coup
Lt. General Olusegun Obasanjo	Feb. 1976– Oct. 1979	Military	West	Peaceful transfer to civilian rule following elections
Alhaji Shehu Shagari	Oct. 1979– Dec.1983	Civilian	North	Deposed by military coup
Major General Muhammadu Buhari	Dec. 1983– Aug. 1985	Military	North	Deposed by military coup
Major General Ibrahim Babangida	Aug. 1985– Aug. 1993	Military	North (middle belt)	Retired in favor of civilian-led interim national government
Chief Ernest Shonekan	Aug.–Nov. 1993	Civilian	West	Deposed by military coup
General Sani Abacha	Nov. 1993– Jun. 1998	Military	North	Reportedly died of heart attack
Major General Abdulsalam Abubakar	Jun. 1998–	Military	North (middle belt)	—

Source: Naomi Chazan, et al., *Politics and Society in Contemporary Africa,* 2d ed. (Boulder, Colo.: Lynne Rienner Publishers, 1992).

and led by Major General Aguiyi Ironsi, castigated the civilian rulers for corruption, fraud, and arrogance.[4] They transformed Nigeria from a federation into a unitary state and declared an intention to return to civilian rule. The composition of the junta and the circumstances of the coup intensified ethnic antipathies, and in July 1966 a group of northern and middle-belt elements in the military staged a countercoup, assassinating General Ironsi and purging Igbos from the government and military ranks.

The army chief of staff, Lt. Colonel Yakubu Gowon, a Christian from the middle belt, assumed leadership of the new regime. Gowon reestablished the federal system while attempting to diffuse the monolithic ethnic blocs through political decentralization. The government subdivided the four regions into twelve states, initiated a revision of the constitution, and repeated a commitment to restore democracy. The second coup, however, aggravated resentments among Nigeria's ethnic communities. Pogroms had been carried out against Igbo enclaves in the north in the wake of the first coup, and a new spate of violence prompted a mass exodus of Igbo civilians and military personnel to their regional homeland. In May 1967, Lt. Colonel Emeka Ojukwu led Igbo officers and political leaders in repudiating the authority of Lagos and declaring the secession of the Biafran Republic. Thus began a bitter civil war in which as many as two million lives were lost to war and famine.

The events of the 1960s established a series of leitmotives that have appeared in subsequent moments of Nigerian politics. These factors continue to influence the perceptions and strategies of political leaders. The competition among Hausa-Fulani, Igbo, and Yoruba political blocs was evident during the Second Republic and has animated other political struggles. This contention is often associated with specific parties and personalities, but it is also expressed in more latent fashion. The recurrent control of the federal executive by leaders aligned with a broad northern Muslim establishment has also been a chronic source of resentment among many southern, eastern, and western groups and political forces. Although political alignments and institutions have undeniably become more complex and varied over the years, these basic fault lines continue to influence alliances and oppositions. The intermittent attempts by northern and eastern politicians to create pragmatic alliances have yielded few lasting effects in reducing the turbulence of communal politics.

In addition, the tactics of electoral manipulation, fraud, violence, and patronage have regularly sullied the conduct of civilian politics in Nigeria, with familiar consequences for legitimacy and stability. The coups of 1966 established precedents not only for the military's role in politics but also for the mode and rationale of military government. Throughout Nigeria's civil-military cycles, nearly all military rulers have presented themselves as caretakers and have legitimized their role by promising transition to a constitutional order. In addition, military rule has often been comparatively liberal in the sense of permitting considerable associational activity, media independence, and even political debate.

The cataclysmic events of the civil war have a singular place in Nigerian history, and the threat of state breakdown remains a salient concern of elites and citizens alike. Civil violence, especially when it is clearly animated by ethnic feeling, still inspires foreboding about broader national instability. Signs of division within civilian and military elites prompt similar fears. The founding era of Nigerian politics left a profound legacy.

THE 1970s: SOLDIERS AND OIL[5]

The civil war ended in January 1970. The ensuing decade was marked by authoritarian rule, a momentous economic transformation, and important alterations in the federal system. Military leaders eventually ceded power to a new democratic government, although the course of the transition was fitful and uncertain. Efforts to achieve political reform unfolded against a backdrop of profound social and economic changes as a petroleum boom transformed the magnitude of government finances and drastically enlarged the domestic market. These developments had far-reaching effects on inequality, social divisions, and the relations of citizens to government.

General Gowon earned popular affirmation for preserving the federation. The regime's postwar policy of national reconciliation helped to restore morale in the aftermath of a devastating conflict. The government echoed its promise to restore civilian rule, although it was nearly a year before a transition agenda was forthcoming. The regime outlined a six-year process of constitutional revision, administrative reform, anticorruption efforts, a reorganization of the armed forces, the revival of party organization, and elections. The political program was accompanied by plans for economic reconstruction and an ambitious, new five-year development scheme.

These aspirations, especially in the economic sphere, were encouraged by the rapid growth of petroleum revenues during the early 1970s. In the late 1960s, major exploration and production activities by foreign firms gained momentum in Nigeria. Petroleum output accelerated rapidly after the civil war, surpassing two million barrels per day in 1973. Nigeria joined the Organization of Petroleum Exporting Countries (OPEC) in 1971, the same year the state oil company was established. The OPEC-inspired price hikes of 1973–74 engendered a threefold rise in export revenues within a year. By the mid-1970s the petroleum sector provided a third of Nigeria's gross domestic product, 80 percent of government finances, and more than 90 percent of the country's export proceeds.

The oil windfall prompted enormous changes in Nigeria's political economy. The rents from oil exports accrued directly to the government, fostering a marked centralization of state resources and fiscal policy. The difficulties of taxation were suddenly eclipsed by struggles over distribution, and a bounteous state was beset with pressures for spending and patronage.[6] The federal system was subject to new challenges as sectional groups agitated for the creation of additional states and the adjustment of revenue allocation formulas. The rise in income was matched by an equally rapid expansion of government activities, fostering enormous waste, inefficiency, and corruption. The frantic growth of the bureaucracy and government-owned companies, and the virtual absence of scrutiny over public spending, afforded wide opportunities to capture public largesse.

The oil boom also created wrenching changes in the private economy and the fabric of Nigerian society. The windfall sparked rising inflation from an overheated economy and rapid urbanization as rural residents flocked to the cities. Widening social inequalities bred crime and tension. The expanding domestic market, fueled by an overvalued exchange rate and the influx of cash, stimulated activities ranging from construction and trade to real estate speculation and wholesale fraud. Because of adverse prices and policies, capital flight was rampant, and few entrepreneurs invested in agriculture or manufacturing enterprises. The era of "pirate capitalism" yielded meager benefits for long-term development.[7]

General Gowon's early political capital was soon exhausted in the face of mounting corruption and delays over important policies. His military governors ran the twelve states like private fiefdoms, and the federal government was rife with misconduct. The cement scandal of 1975, when senior military officers imported massive, excess volumes of cement in order to rake off public funds, was an affront to public opinion. The resulting logjam at the ports provided a vivid sign of avarice in the public sector. In October of that year, Gowon announced that the transition program would be extended indefinitely. While promising constitutional reform, new states, and changes in the governorships, he made no headway in the following months. In July 1975 Gowon was overthrown in a bloodless coup while traveling abroad. Brigadier Murtala Mohammed, a Muslim from Kano and a key figure in the July 1966 revolt, became head of state.

Murtala's combination of populist reform and economic nation-alism galvanized the nation during the heady days of petroleum wealth.[8] Murtala vowed a prompt return to civilian government, and he quick-ly elaborated a four-year transition agenda. He ousted Gowon's mili-tary governors and launched a sweeping purge of the civil service. The government also pushed ahead with an increasingly ambitious program of public spending and state-led industrialization. In February 1976 Murtala was assassinated in an unsuccessful coup attempt. He was suc-ceeded by his chief of staff, Olusegun Obasanjo, a Yoruba Muslim who vowed to preserve his policies. General Obasanjo, aided by his chief of staff, Shehu Yar'Adua, adhered to the transition program and engi-neered Nigeria's first voluntary transfer from military rule to a consti-tutional civilian order.

In addition to implementing political reform, the Murtala-Obasanjo regime also carried out changes in the federal system and expanded the public economy. The creation of seven new states further divided the major regional blocs and provided greater representation for minority ethnic groups. Alterations in the federal revenue allocation formula established new rules for apportioning central resources. In addition, the government affirmed a commitment to move the nation-al capital from Lagos to Abuja, an ethnically neutral location in the center of the country.

The political program commenced in 1975 with the creation of a constitutional drafting committee. The committee's recommendations, delivered the following year, were then debated by an elected con-stituent assembly that convened in 1977. Among the more contentious debates in the constitutional reform process was the status of Islamic shari'a law in the nation's judicial system. This was resolved through a conciliatory arrangement in which predominantly Muslim states could employ shari'a in appropriate areas.

The new constitution, formally adopted in 1979, supplanted par-liamentary institutions with an American-style presidential system. In addition to an executive presidency, the charter provided for a bicameral legislature, an independent judiciary, and an expanded federal structure based on nineteen states. Rules governing political parties and elections were intended to discourage the formation of ethnic or regional associ-ations. Parties were required to follow the principle of a federal charac-ter, demonstrating a balanced representation from all areas of the country.[9] In a formula designed to guarantee broad appeal, the constitu-tion specified that a winning national candidate must garner at least 25 percent of the vote in two-thirds of the states. Ambiguities in this clause

prompted a challenge to the results of the transitional election, as opponents of the winning party claimed it had fallen short of the required voting distribution. The case, although resolved by the Supreme Court,
tarnished the legitimacy of the emerging Second Republic.

When political party activity recommenced in September 1978,
dozens of groups came forward for certification by the Federal Electoral
Commission (FEDECO). This throng was quickly pared down to five
parties that met the exacting criteria for registration; these five con-
tested the 1979 elections (see Table 3.1). In spite of the innovative
political framework, the leading parties and coalitions of the Second
Republic reflected many of the personal, ethnic, and ideological allegiances of the preceding civilian regime.[10]

The Unity Party of Nigeria (UPN), headed by Obafemi Awolowo
(former leader of the western Action Group), mirrored the earlier AG
with its electoral base in the Yoruba states of the southwest. The
Nigerian People's Party (NPP), led by Nnamdi Azikiwe, drew upon
substantial Igbo support in the eastern states. Its programs and constituents were similar to those of the old NCNC. Alhaji Aminu Kano
led the People's Redemption Party (PRP), which appealed to much of
the northern populist constituency that had backed the NEPU. The
UPN, NPP, and PRP embodied more or less radical variants of the populist ideologies of preceding decades. The Great Nigerian People's Party
(GNPP), a breakaway from the NPP led by Alhaji Waziri Ibrahim,
gained a base in the northeastern states.

The National Party of Nigeria (NPN), however, quickly emerged
as the leading competitor. The NPN was a centrist party, claiming a
solid base among former NPC politicians, northern business elites, and
the traditional aristocracy. Despite southern accusations of sectional
bias, the NPN quickly emerged as the most viable party on the basis of
organizational spread and electoral appeal. It became the first party in
Nigeria to create a truly national profile, and these attributes afforded
it success in the 1979 elections. The NPN's Shehu Shagari was elected
president, and the party captured a plurality in the National Assembly
along with control of seven state governments.

THE SECOND REPUBLIC: 1979–83

The Second Republic began under a cloud of controversy as the presidential election yielded a marginal victory for the NPN, which was
upheld in an expedient Supreme Court decision.[11] This was a portentous

moment, since it signaled for many a return to the politics of winner take all in which the ruling federal party would use any available means to consolidate its dominance.[12] Political competition, although structured by a new institutional and legal framework, soon took on familiar traits of acrimony and zero-sum contention.

The early years of the Second Republic witnessed a series of political maneuvers as intricate as those of the 1960s. The NPN and the eastern-based NPP initially formed a partnership of convenience that was loosely countered by a coalition of progressive governors from the southwestern-based UPN, the northern-populist PRP, and the northeastern GNPP. The NPP soon fell out with the NPN establishment, and elements of the NPP affiliated with the opposition. To some degree these alignments reflected ideological distinctions between populist and conservative perspectives, as well as multiethnic resistance to the dominance of a perceived northern establishment party. It was apparent, however, that the commotion of party politics had as much to do with local rivalries and individual posturing as with programmatic or sectional concerns.

As the tactics of political competition grew increasingly brazen and aggressive, the fundamental rules of the game, so integral to stable democratic competition, were quickly discarded. Contending groups bypassed constitutional standards and resorted to open conflict. The use of legal and procedural maneuvers against rivals was evident in conflicts between the NPN and the northern PRP governors. Widespread party defections or carpet crossings also reflected the opportunism of political allegiances. More damaging to the democratic system was the prevalence of electoral fraud and violence. Opposing parties inflated voters' rolls, falsified ballots, bribed voters, tampered with counting procedures, and hijacked the ballots of rivals. Party youth wings and other armed groups intimidated voters and poll watchers and attacked candidates and activists. Hundreds of deaths were attributed to political violence during the second civilian regime.

An unprecedented scale of corruption also tainted the system. The Second Republic straddled the peak years of the petroleum boom, and the copious revenues fueled massive venality among the country's political elites.[13] The claims on public resources multiplied as thousands of politicians and cronies sought favors and contracts or merely siphoned public funds to private accounts. The lively and increasingly partisan media reported numerous exposés and inquiries into the conduct of public officials. These scandals involved hundreds of millions, and possibly billions, of naira, the Nigerian currency. Umaru Dikko, head of the

Presidential Task Force on Rice, was reputedly a billionaire by the end of Shagari's first term. The audacity of such misconduct was displayed in a series of fires in public buildings intended to destroy evidence of illegal activities. In 1981 the tallest building in Lagos, the headquarters of the national telecommunications company, was gutted by such a blaze.

Public resentment over the avarice of the political class deepened as the economy declined. Nigeria's oil revenues reached an apex in 1980 and then decreased sharply with global prices and demand. Government income dropped by nearly half between 1980 and 1982. As the economy slumped, inflation remained high, unemployment and poverty worsened, and public services deteriorated. Widening social disparities fostered restiveness and violence.

Shagari's administration was incapable of implementing necessary adjustments. The NPN machine was fueled by politically driven spending, and fiscal reform was hindered by the continual demands of patronage and electoral expenses. The ambitious economic programs of the boom era also sustained large expenditures.[14] The government's erratic and halfhearted austerity measures failed to cut spending in line with income, and rising deficits were covered by foreign borrowing. As debts accumulated rapidly in the early 1980s, Nigeria confronted a fiscal crisis.

These factors converged in the 1983 elections. Six parties were in contention, as the radical National Advance Party (NAP), led by Tunji Braithwaite, a maverick Lagos attorney, joined the existing pack. A disorderly and increasingly violent campaign incited friction throughout the country. Corruption and frantic disbursements of public largesse to influential interests deepened public disaffection from the political class. The NPN swept the elections, capturing the presidency, an absolute majority in both the House and the Senate, and thirteen state governorships. The magnitude of these results was implausible in view of the inflated voters' register, the NPN's widespread victories recorded in opposition strongholds, and the abundant evidence of electoral misconduct reported by the press and election observers. Sporadic violence erupted in the southwestern states where NPN candidates had defeated popular UPN aspirants. The unrest evoked the events of 1965 that had ruined the First Republic.

The second Shagari administration embarked upon a new term with promises to improve political conduct and rejuvenate the economy. The regime's credibility was nullified by the elections, however, and the Second Republic was terminated at the end of 1983 in a peaceful coup that installed Major General Muhammadu Buhari, a Muslim from Daura, as head of state. In retrospect, the failure of the Second

Republic can be attributed to a somewhat different set of problems from those that had undermined the first civilian regime.[15] While the First Republic succumbed to ethnic contention and institutional flaws, the Second Republic actually possessed a better design and somewhat more diffuse political competition. The effects of the oil boom were probably more fateful for the course of the government. The unmanageable struggle over centralized state resources and the ruthless forms of political conflict scuttled the foundations of competitive politics.

THE RETURN OF THE MILITARY: 1983–85

The 1983 coup d'etat was initially welcomed by much of the Nigerian public. In the early months of the regime General Buhari and his close associate, Major General Tunde Idiagbon, took a number of dramatic steps to curtail political corruption and impose accountability on the civilian political class.[16] Dozens of politicians were arrested and investigated, and a number of prominent officeholders received lengthy prison terms for financial misconduct. The military government also attempted to restore a measure of social order and civility to an unruly public arena.

In the economic realm, however, the Buhari-Idiagbon leadership proved little more adept than its predecessors. While successfully imposing a degree of fiscal austerity, the regime had few means of reviving production or restructuring the country's large foreign debt. Talks with the multilateral financial institutions, which had started in 1983, soon bogged down over the government's refusal to consider key economic policy changes. The economy stagnated in the absence of basic reform of the domestic economy or its international financial position.

The initial enthusiasm that had greeted the Buhari government soon palled as repression and economic drift set in. The unchecked role of the internal security agencies, a heavy-handed attitude toward the media, and reticence about the possibility of another civilian transition all contributed to public malaise. There were many expressions of relief when the regime fell to another military intervention.

THE BABANGIDA REGIME: 1985–93

In August 1985, Major General Ibrahim Babangida took power in a largely bloodless coup. The new president, a Muslim from Niger State, near Abuja, initially displayed a refreshing combination of openness and reform. He promised to reinstate democracy within five years and to liberalize and revive the economy. In the early years of the regime these commitments were advanced by the general's political adeptness and fairly consistent policy measures. During his first year in power Babangida implemented a far-reaching Structural Adjustment Program (SAP) with the support of the World Bank and the International Monetary Fund.[17] He also appointed a political bureau to recommend a plan for transition to a Third Republic. After accepting the body's report in 1987, Babangida asserted that it would be necessary to extend the 1990 transition deadline by two years in order to carry through an effective transfer.[18]

The government's program contained provisions for constitutional change, political party registration, a national census, and a sequence of local and national elections. A new constituent assembly revised the constitutional framework in 1988 and 1989, adhering to clear limits set by the regime. The forum retained presidential institutions and a bicameral legislature but shifted to a legally mandated two-party structure and a stronger role for local governments. The framework also established a formally independent electoral commission and a program of civic education.

Throughout the course of the transition, the Babangida government restricted political participation, the range of debate, and the field of competition.[19] In early 1989 the government lifted the ban on political party activity, and the arena was quickly occupied by numerous parties, six of which received grudging acceptance from the National Electoral Commission (NEC). The regime responded by proscribing all independent political associations and creating instead two official parties. The center-left Social Democratic Party (SDP) and the center-right National Republican Convention (NRC) received official manifestos and organizational charters (see Table 3.1). These authorized parties provided the framework for competitive politics throughout the transition period. Civilian politicians who had served in previous civilian regimes were initially prohibited from participation and then partially readmitted in 1991.

A failed coup attempt in April 1990, followed shortly by a fresh oil revenue windfall, prompted a marked change in Babangida's policies. The unsuccessful army revolt, led by junior officers from the middle-belt states, with backing from a businessman from the Bendel state, threatened a sectional rift within the army and a potentially destructive national conflict. The rebels were subdued within hours, and in the following months Babangida pursued a bloody purge within the military. The regime also imposed more intrusive control on the democratization program and hesitated further in advancing a transition agenda.

The petroleum windfall arrived in the latter half of 1990 as the Gulf crisis raised international oil prices. The sudden bounty provided new resources for economic stabilization and political patronage. In the wake of the miniboom many economic reform measures slackened, although a semblance of adjustment policies was retained. Reckless government spending, spiraling corruption, and delinquent debt service hindered growth while damaging the country's international standing.

Political competition during the transition period echoed the discord of preceding civilian regimes. Public office was again treated as a route to personal and ethnic gratification, and contending political factions employed fraud, patronage, and violence to gain advantage.[20] Internal power struggles and sectional tensions intensified as the schedule proceeded from local government contests to elections for state and national posts. In August 1991, Babangida unexpectedly announced the creation of nine new states and dozens of new local governments. The ensuing administrative confusion created a rationale for a second postponement of the transition date, this time from October 1992 to January 1993. Presidential primaries in August and September 1992 degenerated into wrangling and legal challenges, whereupon the president voided the results and banned all participating candidates from further contesting the vote. For the third time since assuming power, Babangida moved back the democratization deadline. He scheduled a new nomination process for the following spring, set to culminate with presidential elections on June 12. The final transition date was designated as August 27, 1993, the eighth anniversary of Babangida's initial coup d'état.

This deferral fueled mounting popular suspicion that the general harbored a hidden agenda to sustain military rule indefinitely. In an effort to assuage these concerns, Babangida appointed a civilian transitional council in January 1993 to assume routine governmental responsibilities until the August transfer. The transitional council was headed by Ernest Shonekan, a prominent Yoruba business executive. With little political experience and no clear mandate, Shonekan's council, despite its technocratic composition, was basically consigned to a caretaker role.

THE JUNE 12 CRISIS

The presidential election of June 12, 1993, was the last step in the transition schedule prior to the August handover date. During the early months of 1993 the National Electoral Commission (NEC) supervised a complicated nomination process involving an array of party caucuses and votes among local and national constituencies. The two presidential candidates selected by the parties in March were consummate insiders with close connections to military and business elites. Their nominations bore an implicit stamp of acceptance from the regime. The SDP candidate, Bashorun M. K. O. Abiola, was a prominent Yoruba Muslim business figure based in Lagos. Alhaji Bashir Tofa, the NRC nominee, was another Muslim business magnate from the northern Hausa heartland of Kano.

The nominations introduced a new dimension of sectional politics into the presidential contest. Despite perennial discussions of zoning and alternation among different regional candidates, few observers believed that northern elites would relinquish political control. Yet Abiola's candidacy raised a real possibility that a southerner might attain the presidency of the Third Republic. Abiola was a prominent media baron and philanthropist, with national prestige in the Muslim community and extensive personal connections. He bolstered this appeal by selecting Babagana Kingibe, a northern Muslim and former SDP party chairman, as his running mate. Tofa, by contrast, was little-known even in his own constituency. The two-party system, although artificially contrived by the regime, also created the possibility of new, cross-cutting ethnic and regional alignments.

The brief presidential campaign was notably restrained. Public apathy and fatigue dampened interest in the transition, and the politicians sought to avoid giving pretense for additional delays. Consequently, there was little evidence of the contentious politics and misconduct of previous polls. The election was, however, clouded by a series of legal challenges launched by civilian advocates of military rule. The Association for a Better Nigeria (ABN), led by Chief Arthur Nzeribe, had campaigned for a continuation of Babangida's administration, and many observers regarded Nzeribe as a proxy for the designs of senior officers. Two days before the presidential poll, the ABN won an injunction against the election from the Abuja High Court. Although the military regime promptly overruled the court, confusion about the election reduced public participation.

The June 12 elections nonetheless passed without major incident. Although the 35 percent turnout was light, the polling was calm, and participants reported few instances of misconduct or disruption. Administrative and logistical problems abounded, but there was little evidence of systematic fraud or vote rigging and virtually no violence. The election was not formally overseen by external observers, but the independent press and thousands of party monitors generally ratified the exercise. The poll offered an encouraging change from Nigeria's difficult electoral history, and public expectations were high in the days following June 12.

Election returns were quickly tabulated by the NEC, and results leaked to the press indicated a solid 58 percent margin of victory for Chief Abiola.[21] In addition to his base of support in the Yoruba heartland, the SDP candidate also carried important northern, middle-belt, and southeastern states. However transient these results, the electoral outcome signaled a possible shift away from the sectional voting patterns of the past and toward a stronger ideological orientation.

The widespread hopes for a legitimate transition, however, were soon disappointed. Shortly after the election, the ABN obtained a further injunction against release of the results. This prompted a flurry of contradictory rulings from other courts. Eleven days after the poll the government broke its silence on the matter, annulling the election and suspending the NEC. Babangida justified the decision on the grounds that legal and administrative problems had irreparably tainted the process. For many Nigerians, the general's professed concerns for the rule of law rang hollow. As was widely reported, the judge who ruled on the ABN lawsuits had close personal ties to the first lady and had been hastily appointed to the bench in Abuja only weeks earlier. It also seemed highly insincere for a military regime that ruled by decree to announce a sudden responsibility to respect judicial integrity.

The invalidation of the June 12 results tapped a reservoir of discontent, most acutely in the southwestern portion of the country. The perception of disfranchisement by a northern Muslim elite (for the third time since independence) incited deep resentments in Abiola's home region. Many Yorubas believed that ethnic exclusion was the real motive behind the election annulment. Despite initial caution, rioting erupted in Lagos and other southwestern cities within weeks of the annulment. The police responded with force, killing at least a hundred people and prompting wider apprehension. Recalling the strife that foreshadowed the civil war, many southern ethnic groups fled back to their home regions. The government sought to quell the unrest while offering few specific proposals for the transfer of power.

Dissent against the military regime was loosely organized. A tenuous combination of human rights groups, constituents of organized labor, professional associations, elements of the media, students, and fragments of the political parties mobilized in support of democratic rule. The SDP called for a strike in the aftermath of the cancellation, but the leading labor confederation, the Nigerian Labour Congress, was reluctant to lend its support. Babangida displayed his usual skill at disarming opponents by balancing vague promises for new elections with intensified repression.

The international response to the transition crisis was ambiguous. The United States and Great Britain censured the Babangida regime over the annulment and called for a rapid return to democracy. These countries, along with the European Union and Canada, also suspended most nonhumanitarian aid to Nigeria. Chief Abiola spent several weeks in Washington and London to seek support for his mandate. He garnered sympathy but few concrete commitments. Nigeria's other leading trading partners, including France, Germany, and Japan, proved diffident. African governments and regional organizations were generally silent on the unfolding predicament.

Public indignation, pressures from foreigners, and the urgings of some fellow officers finally induced Babangida to vacate office. In late August he hastily departed the presidency and resigned his military commission, turning over authority to a civilian-led interim national government led by Chief Shonekan, the head of the transitional council. Shonekan's appointment as head of state was widely regarded as ceremonial since General Sani Abacha, a Babangida confidant and former chief of staff, was appointed defense minister. The imposition of Abacha on the interim government by Babangida represented an implicit military veto, and many believed that Abacha was positioned to safeguard the interests of military elites or even to exercise direct control over major government decisions.

ENTER ABACHA: NOVEMBER 1993–SEPTEMBER 1994

Throughout the brief period of the interim national government civilian and military leaders maneuvered for advantage. Shonekan announced a series of measures to resume the transition process and advance economic reform. He planned new elections for February 1994, released prominent human rights activists from detention, and suggested a withdrawal of Nigerian forces from an unpopular peacekeeping mission in Liberia. The government's economic team pressed for a resumption of talks with the IMF and the World Bank and prepared for a removal of subsidies on domestic petroleum products, long a sticking point in negotiations with the multilateral lenders. Meanwhile, General

Abacha asserted his own influence through a purge of Babangida loyalists from senior military and intelligence posts.

In a matter of weeks, Abacha exercised full control. The interim government struggled with domestic protest and international censure, displaying little ability to develop a constituency or to implement policy. In an effort to break the impasse with the international financial institutions, Shonekan gambled on the volatile petroleum subsidy issue, announcing a sevenfold increase in fuel prices in early November. The Nigerian Labour Congress promptly launched a general strike that immobilized Lagos and other southern cities. Within three days Abacha forced Shonekan's resignation and took over the levers of government.

General Abacha's palace coup was surrounded by conjecture that he might relinquish power to Abiola or fashion an alternative compromise with the politicians.[22] Instead he abruptly dissolved the elected civilian tiers of government and scrapped the transition framework. His cabinet, however, was comprised mainly of civilians and included a number of prominent politicians. Babagana Kingibe, Abiola's former running mate, surfaced as foreign minister. Several governors and party executives from the Second Republic era were also included, along with a leading human rights activist and one of the country's major independent publishers.

In the early months of his rule, Abacha pursued repressive measures against opposition voices while offering assorted inducements for cooperation. A central forum for the regime's political agenda was the constitutional conference on the framework for a prospective transition. The conference attracted hundreds of politicians and notables with generous government stipends and implied opportunities for future political position. The incorporation of civilians into the cabinet and the constitutional conference, along with other forms of patronage, brought much of the political class into compliance with the regime.

The government adopted a damaging course of economic mismanagement. In January 1994 Abacha discarded the remaining elements of the Structural Adjustment Program and enacted a populist economic package.[23] Government controls on trade, foreign exchange, and domestic prices sent the economy into a steep decline. These policies were accompanied by evidence of massive official corruption and a growing web of international drug trafficking and commercial fraud. The return of authoritarian rule, along with persistent economic impropriety and illegal activities, set off a new round of international penalties affecting air links, visas, sports activities, and assistance from multilateral donors.

The initial opposition response to Abacha's government was divided and uncertain. The dissolution of the SDP depleted Abiola's political organization, and he had difficulty in mobilizing active support beyond the southwestern portions of the country. As a politician, Abiola displayed a preference for negotiating directly with the military rather than mobilizing a diverse popular constituency. This created a substantial liability, as important elements of a potential democratic coalition, including northern progressives, organized labor, and many southern notables, felt neglected and were soon estranged from Abiola's leadership. The democratic camp soon divided among those who insisted upon the June 12 mandate as the basis for political transition and a growing segment who were amenable to compromise, possibly including new elections. Abiola and his allies pursued quiet dialogue with the military over a possible transfer of power, but these discussions produced no tangible results.

The pressures for democratization gained momentum in the weeks before the first anniversary of the June 12 election. In May a new organization, the National Democratic Coalition (NADECO), was publicly unveiled. NADECO was a multiethnic group of former politicians, notables, and retired military officers dedicated to advancing Abiola's mandate. The group provided the Abiola circle with a new organizational base, lending substantial weight to renewed demands for a rapid transition.

Abiola launched a new campaign to affirm the verdict of June 12. Shortly before the election anniversary, he publicly challenged the military to abdicate and called for the creation of a shadow cabinet. The regime proscribed NADECO and cautioned against provocative action. On June 11 Abiola declared himself the legitimate president of Nigeria. General Abacha retorted the following evening in an address to the nation that warned against political chaos. Police issued a warrant for the dissident politician, who eluded capture for several days. Although June 12 passed quietly, Abiola resurfaced ten days later to address a public rally, whereupon he was arrested. Within two weeks authorities formally charged Abiola with treason, legally a capital offense.

The confrontation between government and opposition quickly intensified. On July 4 the oil workers' union, the National Union of Petroleum and Natural Gas Employees (NUPENG), initiated a strike to demand Abiola's release and recognition of the June 12 mandate. After the announcement of treason charges against Abiola the Nigerian Labour Congress threatened a general strike in support of NUPENG's demands. The blue-collar oil workers were joined by the

Petroleum and Natural Gas Senior Staff Association (PENGASSAN), the union of senior petroleum employees. The petroleum unions were soon accompanied by disgruntled bank employees and prodemocracy academics as scattered protests and rioting erupted in several southwestern cities.

For nine weeks the petroleum workers' actions paralyzed the nation. At the peak of the strike oil exports were reduced by a third, although revenue losses were lessened by a concurrent increase in world prices.[24] The chief impact was seen in the domestic economy as strikers idled the national fuel distribution system and immobilized the transportation network. The Nigerian Labour Congress briefly joined the strike, but its pliant central leadership was quickly appeased by the government. Nonetheless, the converging protests displayed the most forceful resistance to military rule in Nigerian experience.

The regime subdued the opposition through a mixture of repression and inducement. Abacha moved to end the standoff in mid-August by removing the leadership of the petroleum unions and imposing further authoritarian measures. Following a summary dismissal of union executives, the offices of the unions were sealed and their leaders arrested. The government also shuttered three independent media companies and promulgated a decree exempting itself from the jurisdiction of the courts. A preventive detention order expedited the arrest of democracy activists, while unknown assailants staged attacks on the homes of several prominent dissidents. More than 120 street protesters were killed as security forces quelled disturbances in major cities.

REPRESSION AND CONSOLIDATION: OCTOBER 1994–DECEMBER 1995

By early September the military government had clearly prevailed. Strike activity dissipated, allowing normal activities to resume in the petroleum industry and the financial sector. Chief Abiola, the leaders of the dissident petroleum unions, and a number of other prodemocracy activists remained in detention. In the wake of the strikes Abacha took additional steps to bolster his control. He purged civilians from his ruling council, reshuffled his cabinet, and moved against military personnel whose loyalty was suspect.[25] The government took tentative steps to liberalize the economy, and performance improved slightly. The constitutional conference proceeded, but the government did not act on many of its central recommendations.

In March 1995 the regime announced it had thwarted an attempted coup plot. As many as four hundred officers and civilians were arrested or detained. Among those accused were retired generals Olusegun Obasanjo, the former head of state, and Shehu Musa Yar'Adua, Obasanjo's former chief of staff and a recent presidential aspirant. Obasanjo and Yar'Adua were both vocal critics of military rule, having previously supervised the 1979 transition to the civilian Second Republic. Several prominent journalists were also arrested along with Beko Ransome-Kuti, a leading activist who chaired the Campaign for Democracy. The authenticity of the alleged conspiracy was in considerable doubt, and critics charged that Abacha had inflated or contrived the incident as a pretext to remove further challenges to his authority.[26] Set against a background of continuing restrictions on the media and harassment of democratic activists, Abacha's government represented the most repressive rule in Nigerian history. The combination of centralized power, flagrant corruption, and blunt authoritarianism was unprecedented in Nigerian experience.

Despite these circumstances, Abacha continued to affirm his commitment to eventual democratization. On October 1, 1995, the regime announced a new schedule for transition to civilian rule, set to culminate in precisely three years. The program was modeled on General Babangida's previous agenda, prompting observers to compare Abacha's plan with his predecessor's maneuvers to preserve power. The major differences in the new constitutional framework were the introduction of a six-zone regional classification and a provision for rotation of political candidates among the zones. A complex executive structure including a president, prime minister, vice president, and deputy prime minister was also provided. Appendix E provides the Abacha regime's transition schedule.

The regime conducted in camera trials for more than forty of the alleged coup plotters. The secret tribunal handed down severe rulings, including a death sentence for Yar'Adua and life imprisonment for Obasanjo. The dearth of clear evidence and a lack of due process elicited protests from the United States, Britain, and some of Nigeria's other key trading partners. The government in Abuja responded to international calls for leniency by reducing sentences for several of the alleged coup plotters.[27] Abacha was reportedly offended when he did not receive subsequent calls thanking him for his forbearance.

This perceived slight may have partly motivated the blunt and provocative action against another group of political dissidents. On November 10, 1995, the regime abruptly executed Ken Saro-Wiwa and eight other activists from the Movement for the Survival of the Ogoni People (MOSOP). Saro-Wiwa was a prominent journalist and activist from the Ogoni community of southeastern Nigeria. Ogoniland is located in a central, oil-producing region of the Niger Delta, and since 1990 the Ogoni movement had promoted an increasingly militant campaign against the government and the Royal Dutch/Shell oil company to protest environmental degradation and economic neglect of the area. The government responded to the activities of MOSOP with a heavy police and military occupation of Ogoniland. The movement itself became divided among moderate and radical factions. In 1994 Saro-Wiwa and twenty-seven compatriots were arrested in connection with riots that had killed four progovernment Ogoni chiefs.

Nine of the defendants, including Saro-Wiwa, were arraigned on capital murder charges. Their trial before a special judicial panel was closed to most outside observers, and legal experts challenged the validity of the proceedings. The sudden execution of the Ogoni Nine after a flawed trial and virtually no judicial review provoked a wave of international denunciation.[28] The killing of Saro-Wiwa was particularly shocking in light of his general reputation as a nonviolent intellectual.

The executions occurred during the annual meeting of the Commonwealth Head of Governments summit, which subsequently suspended Nigeria from the Commonwealth. The United States tightened a range of restrictions on travel, aid, and trade with Nigeria and declared that it would give consideration to an oil embargo against the country. The European Union and Canada were also highly critical of the regime, and the United Nations General Assembly began debate on a resolution of censure. Even some of the traditionally reticent African states expressed disapproval: the leaders of Zimbabwe and South Africa reproached the regime for its authoritarian actions. Nigeria was rapidly becoming a pariah in the world community.

ISOLATION AND IMPASSE: DECEMBER 1995–JUNE 1998

After the executions, however, Nigeria's domestic and external circumstances stabilized considerably. Internationally, the Abacha government maintained a tense diplomatic standoff with the Commonwealth, the United Nations, the United States, Canada, and South Africa, which had emerged as Nigeria's most vocal international critics. The regime continued to draw criticism and periodic scrutiny for its human

rights record, along with continuing problems of economic misconduct, corruption, and drug trafficking. Most of the country's major trading partners, however, were averse to stronger sanctions, and
international measures were essentially restricted to verbal and sym-
bolic gestures. The Nigerian government also launched aggressive and
well-funded lobbying efforts in Washington and other international
capitals, and these campaigns showed some effect in easing external
pressures. Commerce and foreign investment proceeded, although a
weak economy and lagging debt service limited the country's access to
external markets and discouraged investment outside the energy sector.

Domestically, overt opposition to the military government abat-
ed substantially. A variety of human rights groups, prodemocracy organizations, and professional and popular associations continued to
protest abuses by the regime and to urge a rapid return to democracy.
Substantial segments of the independent press also continued to operate. These activities existed in a gray zone of semilegality, and the government used decrees, detentions, and occasional violence to subdue
dissident voices, including a spate of arrests and several unexplained
murders of noted political activists. Among the most prominent
killings was that of Kudirat Abiola, the wife of the imprisoned leader,
who was shot along with her driver by a carful of armed men in June
1996 in an area of downtown Lagos saturated with army checkpoints.
Attacks on senior NADECO leaders also had a chilling effect on opposition activity.

When political party organization was authorized in mid-1996
under the official transition program, the regime tightly controlled
the registration process. In October, the government electoral commission accredited five parties, conspicuously excluding groups linked
to opposition politicians. The authorized parties—the United Nigerian
Congress Party (UNCP), the Democratic Party of Nigeria (DPN), the
Congress for National Consensus (CNC), the National Center Party
of Nigeria (NCPN), and the Grassroots Democratic Movement
(GDM)—bore little outward resemblance to previous Nigerian political associations, although a number of veteran politicians appeared as
founding members (see Table 3.1). The striking feature of the new
parties was their nebulous identity. They did not readily correspond to
a clear ethnic or regional makeup, much less a set of ideological distinctions. Although their leadership was strewn with notables, many
prominent veteran politicians were absent, either through exclusion
or apathy. The "newbreed" (as the new parties are often known local-
ly) has been a generally indistinct and untested group. They revealed

the purpose for which they had apparently been formed when all nominated General Abacha as their presidential candidate in April 1998.

A few days after the nominations, on April 25, elections for the national assembly were largely shunned by Nigerian voters. Local observers reported participation rates of less than 5 percent in most areas of the country. In the weeks that followed, a cross section of veteran politicians and other notables, including some prominent northerners, urged the head of state to refrain from contesting the presidency and to allow a fair election. International responses to Abacha's apparent self-succession were negative, though largely restrained.

On June 8, 1998, General Abacha died of a heart attack, according to official reports. His body was quickly moved from the presidential compound in Abuja for interment in his home city of Kano. The day after his death, the Provisional Ruling Council, a military body, named Major General Abdulsalam Abubakar, the chief of defense staff, as the new head of state. General Abubakar affirmed his commitment to a transition to civilian rule and released major political prisoners.

— 4 —

SITUATION REPORT

CPA's study mission to Nigeria in January 1997 sought to examine current conditions in the country, to assess the prospects for democratic reform and conflict resolution, and to consider the role of both international and Nigerian domestic organizations and individual figures in promoting change. On the one hand, General Abacha established the most repressive government in Nigeria's post-independent history. The country's military rulers have governed without accountability, political participation has been stringently curtailed, human rights abuses have been endemic, and the traditionally independent media have been partly curbed. On the other hand, while access to state resources and power has been severely restricted, there is participation, and even limited pluralism, in some areas of public life. State repression is neither comprehensive nor efficient, and there remains a significant gray area of political activity and social mobilization. Nonetheless, most of the population does not enjoy access to the political arena. Coercion, exclusion, and co-optation have been relatively successful at imposing temporary political quiescence. While these strategies have reduced the immediate prospect of large-scale, violent conflict, many deeper, long-term risks continue to threaten Nigeria's stability as a nation-state. Indeed, the exclusionary nature of the regime has magnified these risks.

In contrast with the early years of General Abacha's regime, by 1997 there was less public expression of protest against official programs. The government narrowed the latitude for independent political activity and actively suppressed or bought off the most vigorous elements of political opposition. Many dissident groups were consequently divided, intimidated, exhausted, or exiled. During our trip to Nigeria we observed the restrictive circumstances for opposition organizations, the personal challenges and risks confronted by individual activists, and the difficulties of raising critical voices against government leaders or policies. Nonetheless open mass protest reemerged in 1998 in response to General Abacha's uncontested presidential candidacy and the death sentences imposed on alleged coup plotters. New opposition organizations appeared, and several prominent politicians protested the Abacha candidacy. In the weeks following Abacha's death, domestic and exiled opposition elements urged the government of General Abubakar to release prisoners of conscience, open political life, and adopt democratic reforms. Some organizations, including NADECO, called for the military government to enter into a dialogue over political change. Among the most important questions in Nigeria's immediate future are the relative strength of the democratic movement and the possibilities for effective engagement between government and opposition.

The weakness of opposition activity was portrayed by the Abacha regime and its supporters as a sign that Nigeria is moving down a path of normalization and reform. Beginning in 1995, the government proceeded with a planned transition to civilian rule (scheduled to conclude in 1998) and announced measures to liberalize the economy. Skepticism about the political transition program has been nearly universal among Nigerians, although the economic measures initially earned some guarded approval, even among a few opponents of the government. Among the public at large, the repressive environment, a chronic political cynicism and distrust of politicians that nearly matches their resentment of military rule, and the preoccupations of survival in a depressed economy have fostered general fatigue, leaving scant popular energy for confrontation with the military government. The legacy of the June 12, 1993, elections has also proved divisive. Chief M. K. O. Abiola's supporters both in Nigeria and in exile regard that election as the touchstone of political legitimacy. While such arguments are based on democratic principles, this feeling is most intense in Abiola's native southwest region and among his fellow Yoruba. In other parts of the country we found that even some opponents of the government now perceive June 12 as a Yoruba grievance rather than a purely democratic cause. In addition, it should be noted that some quarters of Nigerian society are comfortable with the political status quo, while others perceive favorable opportunities in the government's political and economic agenda.

The containment of opposition, however, should not obscure the real and continuing hazards of instability in Nigeria. Central government institutions and the broader social fabric show considerable evidence of weakness and dissension. The most visible warning signs have been repeated allegations of coup attempts; a spate of bombings aimed at military personnel, which have extended beyond Lagos to eastern, middle-belt, and northern cities; several killings and assaults targeting prominent opposition figures; regular outbursts of violence among ethnic and religious communities throughout the country; and the extreme disaffection of much of the Yoruba community. In addition, religious strife in northern Nigeria and tensions with minorities in the oil-producing regions reflect the intense antipathy of some popular groups toward government in all regions of the country.

In a more prosaic sense, basic conditions of life are deteriorating markedly for most Nigerians. Violent crime is epidemic, and, despite the attention paid to dissidents, the capabilities of public security forces are weak. Pervasive official corruption has severely undermined the economy and generated widespread popular alienation from government. Major public services including education and health are barely functioning, while electricity and fuel distribution are erratic. The CPA delegation experienced this firsthand, as the guest house where it stayed in a middle-class neighborhood of Lagos relied for power on an electrical generator, which ran for several days at a time. Reports of gasoline scarcities during our stay indicated the beginning of a massive fuel shortage that crippled the country in the months to follow, and lingered into 1998. Economic decline has resulted in increased poverty and insecurity, which in turn aggravate social tensions.

Major sources of instability and conflict in Nigeria remain unresolved. The most salient issue is the feeling in the country's restive western region that the military government and northern elites intend to exclude them permanently from political power. In our discussions there, many people asserted that the 1993 elections were annulled because the northern Nigerian "establishment" could not tolerate a Yoruba, Chief Abiola, as president. Some people even talked of a desire for the partition of Nigeria, to provide the southwest with autonomy from the north. We later spoke with northerners who expressed a belief that southerners were actively scheming to capture the central government as a way of augmenting their existing control of the economy. Such ethno-regional fault lines have incited political upheaval at least three times in Nigeria's postindependence history, and persistent exclusion is likely to yield future problems. In addition, the growing discord in the southern minority areas of the Niger Delta, where most Nigerian oil is produced, also commands attention. Not all of these disturbances are directly aimed at the military regime, but they reflect enmity toward the government, and they have the potential to disrupt Nigeria's leading economic sector.

Ethnic dissension is related to another problem of major importance: the internal cohesion of the military itself. The military differed over Babangida's annulment of the election, and it appeared to be similarly divided over Abacha's transition process. The persistence of factional disputes within the military has been indicated by the large-scale internal purge following accusations of a coup plot in March 1995, and more recently by the December 1997 arrest of eleven senior officers and a civilian, mainly Yorubas, in connection with the regime's allegations of another planned revolt. The possibilities of further military intervention, or even a disintegration of the military into internal conflict, pose significant dangers of instability. Strife among ethnically based military groupings in 1966–67 provided the stimulus for the subsequent Nigerian civil war.

The Abacha government presented its political and economic programs as the means to achieve stability and reconciliation in Nigeria. The study group found little evidence to support this perspective, and we observed increasing signs of instability, rather than indications of accord, as these programs unfolded. We met with considerable skepticism among Nigerians about the credibility of military-led reforms. At a preparatory meeting for the Vision 2010 conference, all of whose participants were screened or appointed by the present government, twelve people were asked to cast five votes each to choose the most crucial issue facing Nigeria. Forty of the sixty votes were for permanent military withdrawal from politics. Opponents of the government and many ordinary Nigerians dismissed Abacha's transition as another pretext to sustain the military in power even before his nomination by all five parties. In the wake of Babangida's abortive, eight-year democratization scheme, there has been widespread frustration with Abacha's extended schedule and increasing cynicism about Nigeria's "permanent transition."[1]

General Abacha's political transition plan never embodied a full transition to democracy. At best it would have created a form of civil-military dyarchy. The program ostensibly established a timetable and institutional machinery for the passage of state power to elected authorities. The government registered five carefully screened political parties. Opposition groups were excluded from competition. The officially controlled electoral commission supervised local government elections in March 1997, polls for state assemblies in December, and elections for the National Assembly in April 1998. The presidential election scheduled for August was evidently rendered moot by Abacha's uncontested candidacy, though gubernatorial elections were also to be held at that time. The draft constitution submitted in 1995 was not published by June 1998, and so the country entered the final months of its transition program without a working constitution. Moreover, the entire "transition" exercise has taken place in an oppressive political environment, which we detail below.

Many Nigerians took part in the local government elections of March 1997, but turnout continually dropped as the transition advanced. It decreased sharply in the December 1997 state assembly polls to about 15 percent of registered voters. The April 1998 national legislative elections seemed to reach new lows, with turnout reliably estimated by reports at about 5 percent.[2]

This indicated a new level of disdain for the official transition program. In the early stages of the program, many aspiring politicians joined the registered political parties. Critics dismissed these activities as a mere scramble over political spoils, but some Nigerians had hoped that the political contest might lead to a gradual political opening. Such expectations were discouraged as the transition proceeded.

In 1998 General Abacha and his regime made key decisions about the course and content of the transition program. Rather than leading the military back to the barracks and liberalizing, General Abacha evidently sought the presidency himself, unopposed, in an attempt to regularize his regime under a civilian mantle. Although General Abacha did not have the opportunity to indicate his political intentions explicitly, senior members of his regime consistently asserted his prerogative to contest the presidency, leaders of the principal government-approved political parties endorsed his candidacy, and staged meetings of state-supported "traditional rulers" and youth groups requested that he run. The possibility of Abacha's entry into the political race evidently kept others at bay, and by the end of 1997 only a single candidate, the gadfly lawyer and activist Tunji Braithwaite, had announced an intention to run for the presidency. In January 1998 former head of the national police Alhaji M. D. Yusufu also indicated an intention to run. Both sought the nomination of the Grassroots Democratic Movement, the most independent of the five parties, but last minute machinations assured Abacha of that nomination as well.

Economic policy is another potential area of change where early promises were not kept. The government shifted from the policy direction of 1993–95, which was not yielding the hoped-for results, and attempted to improve some aspects of macroeconomic performance.

Officials also suggested a number of measures for economic opening, including the promise of a major privatization program. These commitments were supplemented by announcement of efforts to rescue the failing banking system, to improve the administration of government contracts, and to reduce corruption in the customs service and major ports of entry. In our discussions with Nigerian business leaders, these efforts were clearly welcomed, although they pointed out that the business environment had not yet improved. The problems of crime and political instability present additional brakes on business activity. As one business association executive remarked, "A lot of [foreign investors] are keen to come to Nigeria. They see the potential, but they are afraid of instability, and [in]security of life and property."

In addition, the regime encouraged a process of public dialogue on economic policy through participation in the Nigerian Economic Summit, an annual conference organized by representatives of the private sector, and sponsorship of the Vision 2010 seminar, a lengthy program of high-level discussions on Nigerian development convened in 1996 and 1997. Discussion in these forums has been lively, as the CPA delegation observed when it attended a Vision 2010 seminar in January 1997. Debate extended across a broad array of issues pertaining to economic policy and administration. Nevertheless, these discussions failed to attract the credibility they might otherwise deserve because several essential topics have been off-limits, including the role of the military and the representation of popular groups. Controversial aspects of governance and democracy, which are integrally related to the quality of economic management, have generally been avoided. Even with these faults, such initiatives still represent a step toward greater consultation between government and the private sector. They have provided an outlet for leading advocates of improved economic management, although the acid test of these efforts obviously lies in their implementation. In a different political environment, they could be useful.

Alongside the various initiatives at the official level, it is also important to recognize the considerable, ongoing activity within Nigeria's nongovernmental sector. In the face of substantial restrictions on participation, a variety of civic organizations continue to operate in Nigeria, and many have persisted in pressuring the government to respect human rights and carry out a genuine transition to democracy. Civil society organizations can provide an important antidote to the prevailing political cynicism in Nigeria, and they offer the strongest links to broad constituencies at the grass roots. Despite political and economic constraints, a number of organizations provide services to clients along with public

advocacy of sundry interests. Business organizations provide a prominent example, but a number of women's groups and community associations, religious and professional organizations, the independent media,
and even human rights advocates remain active. Trade unions, which
were very important in the past, have largely been repressed and brought
under government control, but with the release from prison of major
labor leaders after Abacha's death, perhaps they will revive.

These groups offer a potential source of pressure on government
for improved political, economic, and social conditions. They involve
people in real issues of representation, welfare, or development that
have generally been neglected by both military leaders and politicians.
As such, they drive the popular demand for accountability in Nigeria.
Within Nigeria's potentially fractious society, nongovernmental organizations can also promote conflict resolution and accord. If the state dis-
regards the interests of societal groups, however, the results can be
destabilizing. As a senior Nigerian academic observed with regard to
the ongoing political crisis, "I don't see the end of conflict unless the government engages with civil society." Moreover, many civic associations
are linked to international networks of civil society that complement
groups within Nigeria. Professionals, business, women's associations,
human rights and environmental organizations, and many religious communities have close ties to external organizations and movements. The
roles and capacities of civil society are elaborated in the next chapter.

With these general questions and conclusions in mind, we turn to
a fuller discussion of Nigeria's current political, economic, and social
conditions. In the account that follows, we consider fundamental, long-
term challenges to stability and development in Nigeria, along with
more immediate hazards arising from the recent political crisis and the
nature of military rule.

THE CLOSURE OF POLITICS: REPRESSION

A defining feature of the Nigerian situation from 1993 until the death
of General Abacha was the dramatic closure of political space. The latitude for debate, organization, and activity was restricted through overt
controls as well as tacit intimidation. Direct opposition to military rule
was effectively proscribed. Leading political organizations such as the
National Democratic Coalition (NADECO), the Campaign for
Democracy, and the National Conscience Party were stigmatized by
government and virtually driven underground. Their leaders were

arrested, harassed, or physically attacked, and some were publicly accused by the Abacha regime of perpetrating foreign-sponsored terrorist activities. At least two prominent democracy activists—Alfred Rewane, a NADECO leader and patron, and Kudirat Abiola, Chief Abiola's wife—were murdered by unidentified assailants. It is popularly accepted among many in the country that the government was complicit in these killings, and some commentators have alleged the presence of officially sanctioned "hit squads," an unprecedented activity in Nigeria. This has been accompanied by a continual procession of arrests of opposition figures and a dawdling judicial process that keeps detainees in prison for extended periods.

The most prominent detainees and prisoners have included Chief M. K. O. Abiola, the apparent winner of the 1993 presidential election, who has been detained on treason charges; retired generals Olusegun Obasanjo and (until his death in December 1997) Shehu Musa Yar'Adua, both convicted in secret trials on charges relating to an alleged coup plan; Dr. Beko Ransome-Kuti, a prominent democratic activist, also held for complicity in the purported coup plot; Frank Kokori, deposed head of the oil union NUPENG; his counterpart, Milton Dabibi, leader of the senior oil staff union PENGASSAN; and nineteen members of the Ogoni rights organization, the Movement for the Survival of the Ogoni People (MOSOP). Obasanjo, Yar'Adua, and Ransome-Kuti were convicted by a secret military tribunal in 1995, and the other detainees have been held without trial, some for as long as four years.[3] Yar'Adua did not survive his imprisonment, dying suddenly (many have said suspiciously) at the age of fifty-four. The November 1995 hangings on capital murder charges of MOSOP leader Ken Saro-Wiwa and eight compatriots, after a trial riddled with irregularities, were widely condemned by the international community.[4] In January 1997, twenty-two NADECO supporters were detained in connection with bombings in Lagos, and sixteen persons were subsequently charged with treason, a capital crime. This group included the exiled Nobel laureate Wole Soyinka, who was charged in absentia. The government has produced no evidence for these allegations. In December 1997 the government claimed to have uncovered another coup plot and sentenced sixteen prisoners in April 1998, including six death sentences. Among those sentenced to death was Lieutenant General Oladipo Diya, formerly Abacha's deputy. All those sentenced to death were Yorubas. A week after General Abacha's death in June 1998, the Abubakar regime released Obasanjo, Ransome-Kuti, Kokori, Dabibi, Ibrahim Dasuki (the former sultan of Sokoto), and four other political detainees. Government spokesmen announced that further releases were imminent.

The security establishment also persecuted activists, professionals, and public figures. Dozens of human rights advocates, journalists, lawyers, and religious figures were detained without trial, many for extended periods. Academic dissenters were summarily dismissed from their universities or warned by officials to curb their activities. We met professors in both southwestern and northern universities who had been questioned by security officials or had narrowly escaped arrest. We also discussed the problem of political persecution in the universities with lawyers who had defended these cases. A number of outspoken Nigerians had their passports confiscated by authorities or were subject to long interrogations at the airport when traveling. A few prominent dissidents fled the country clandestinely. In this vein as well we note the anonymous armed assaults that have killed, wounded, or unnerved several opposition figures.[5]

In addition, the scope of political discussion has been controlled by government officials and regulated by a watchful security apparatus. The Abacha regime closely guided its official transition program and cleared five political parties for registration. None of these parties has included any critics of the current government. Outside the formal party framework there has been little room for independent political expression. A human rights advocate remarked to us, "We used to be proud in this country that we could abuse the government and get away with it." This was replaced by a climate of fear as people were arbitrarily arrested, and police checkpoints could detain individuals for carrying unacceptable political literature.

The press operates in limbo. Independent media outlets continue to function, and many report on sensitive topics. When they cross an invisible line of acceptability, however, the government has confiscated editions, closed offices, and detained staff. Editors and reporters enter and leave prison through a revolving door of detentions and releases. Several publications have been shuttered, and a few have been vandalized.

The study group encountered a chilling political environment, especially in Lagos and Ibadan. Opposition elements, human rights groups, journalists, women's advocates, and many professional associations work under severe constraints. The Academic Staff Union of Universities (ASUU) has been formally banned, and the leading labor organizations, with their leaders deposed or in detention, are managed by government administrators. Most activist groups assume that they are infiltrated by the security agencies. Numerous public meetings have been closed or disrupted, including many that were not overtly political. One prominent example was the September 1997 raid by Lagos police on a Nigerian farewell party for U.S. ambassador Walter Carrington. Dissident religious groups in the northern states have been abruptly suppressed. The pall of state repression was clearly greater in the southern portions of Nigeria, and particularly in the southwest. In the north, where many civil society organizations are relatively weaker or organized differently, repression is directed more against grassroots Islamic movements.

The ubiquitous presence of security personnel is also a source of incessant petty abuses against common citizens. Taking government concerns over crime and terrorism as a rationale, police and military checkpoints are prevalent on major thoroughfares in much of the country. These units operate with little accountability, and residents are commonly subject to searches, demands for bribes, and other mistreatment. The justifiable presence of law enforcement has in many places deteriorated into a situation of crude and increasingly brazen extortion. We were personally acquainted with this aspect of Nigerian life on the evening we arrived in Lagos, when we were stopped by an armed police checkpoint just outside the airport. After searching our luggage and frisking the members of our group for more than thirty minutes, the officers demanded increasing amounts of money to let us pass and threatened to arrest us if payment was not made. We were relieved of about $170 and permitted to go only when a well-connected friend arrived to intervene with the police. In recounting this episode during our trip, we discovered that virtually every Nigerian we spoke to had a similar tale. While we did not experience another "shakedown" of this sort, our cars were repeatedly stopped by police and military checkpoints, which were often quite aggressive. We observed that these problems were more pronounced in Lagos than in the northern cities of Kano, Kaduna, or Abuja.

THE POLITICAL CLASS: RIVALRY AND CO-OPTATION

A few civilian politicians, notably Chief Abiola and the exiled senator Bola Tinubu, have experienced the brunt of military persecution. In general, however, professional politicians have not suffered from widespread repression. Instead, the effectiveness of the civilian political class—including former politicians and new aspirants—has been dissipated in factionalism, rivalry, and co-optation by the government. Divisions arise from ethnic and regional distinctions, personal ambition, and a degree of ideological contention. These fissures are intensified by a system whereby politicians compete as much, if not more, for support from military rulers as from the voters. Political factions jockeyed intensely within the government-sanctioned parties during Babangida's transition, and a similar commotion has been evident in the parties under Abacha's program. Such wrangling shows little connection to political programs or policy alternatives, and few of the potential candidates enjoy any substantial popular base. Moreover, party organizations have been largely separated from civil society groups as the politicians compete within their own rarefied domain, which is effectively divorced from actual governance.

In the wake of the 1993 transition crisis, the politicians displayed little capacity to apply concerted pressure on the government or to advance a common program of political demands, and many have since been amenable to cooperation with the military. Perhaps the most conspicuous example is that of Babagana Kingibe, Chief Abiola's vice presidential running mate, who accepted a post as foreign minister in Abacha's first cabinet and later rotated to other cabinet posts. This, however, is but one of many instances where politicians have served in the military government, participated in the official constitutional conference, or joined the government-sanctioned political parties. Given the tumultuous history of civilian politics in Nigeria, a broad spectrum of the public is understandably skeptical about the ability of the politicians to establish an enduring democratic system. Although much of the Nigerian public clearly harbors democratic aspirations, its evident disenchantment with the political class has only added to the cynicism engendered by the military's control of the "transition" process. This pessimism likely contributed to the sparse voter turnout witnessed in the December 1997 state legislative elections and the sparser turnout in the April 1998 national legislative elections.

On a national scale the regime has sought alliances with selected northern notables, conspicuous Igbo figures, representatives from middle-belt areas, and a few Yorubas in an effort to broaden the government's geographic acceptance. At the same time, authorities have sought to isolate dissenters by playing upon regional anxieties. Senior government officials have repeatedly accused southwestern groups of fomenting national discord and have rationalized stern measures by the regime in terms of preserving unity. Abacha referred to the dissidents in the Delta as "unpatriotic Nigerians" in his October 1, 1997, speech. Nigerian elites have privately distributed a clearly fraudulent pamphlet purporting to document a "Yoruba Agenda" to seize power in Nigeria.[6] The December 1997 arrests in connection with an alleged coup plot also mainly targeted Yoruba military officers, and all six subsequently sentenced to death were Yorubas. Such tactics have the effect of polarizing regional blocs and creating apprehension among other southern communities.

UNCERTAINTY WITHIN THE MILITARY

Certainly the most volatile source of division among Nigerian elites is found within the armed forces. In view of their central role in politics as well as internal security, the cohesion and stability of this institution are decisive for the prospects of the nation. The problem of inculcating military professionalism has been crucial to Nigeria's travails in recent decades. Nigeria has a historical precedent of intramilitary disputes resulting in civil war; the 1966 coups and the attempted Biafran secession arose from segmentation in the armed forces. In light of this experience, signs of degeneration within the security apparatus could foretell dangerous consequences for the integrity of the state.

Factionalism among civilian politicians is echoed, if not precisely matched, by segmentation within the security forces. Divisions at the ethnic, regional, and personal levels create sources of insecurity. It is important to bear in mind that the military is vulnerable to the same stresses and divisions that appear in the wider society. Serious popular strife could have a contagion effect on the security institutions, and internal division or upheaval in the military might incite latent conflict in Nigerian society, as occurred in 1967 at the start of the civil war.

There is substantial evidence of discord within the armed forces in recent years. Since 1984, apart from three successful military interventions (those of Buhari, Babangida, and Abacha), there have been two prominent coup attempts, in 1985 and 1990, and two other plots alleged by the Abacha regime, in 1995 and 1997. Rumors of attempted coups also circulate constantly. In recent years the officer corps has been shaken by repeated purges, reshuffles, trials, and executions. The most notorious episodes followed the abortive Vatsa coup of 1985, the failed revolt in 1990, and the alleged conspiracy of 1995. These actions resulted in at least eighty executions and dozens of lengthy prison terms. Since 1995, some 320 army officers have been summarily dismissed or forced to retire, and sixty-four air force officers were sacked in mid-1997. The chiefs of army and naval staff were fired in 1995, and the following year military administrators in the thirty-six states were dismissed.[7] Many senior officers have taken early retirement, some reportedly under duress, and others have been sidelined to obscure postings. The consequence is an atmosphere of distrust and division, prompting concerns about the erosion of professionalism and the danger of reckless actions by ambitious military factions. There have been suggestions that recent bombings against soldiers reflect intramilitary rivalries, although the attacks have not been definitively traced. Some reports indicated that Abacha did not trust any units other than his own presidential detachment.[8]

On December 21, 1997, Lieutenant General Oladipo Diya, the deputy head of state, was arrested along with eleven others, most of whom were senior officers of Yoruba ethnicity. Officials of the regime alleged that the group was the core of a conspiracy to overthrow the Abacha government. As in the case of the alleged 1995 coup plot, the regime was slow to produce evidence in support of its allegations, although groups of northern traditional rulers and foreign diplomats were privately presented with some corroboration in the form of video-taped confessions. On April 28, a closed military tribunal handed down death sentences for six of the defendants, including General Diya, and long prison terms for ten others. Thirteen defendants were acquitted. Whether or not these charges were valid, they indicate deep divisions within the military establishment and the chronic insecurity of the leaders in Aso Rock, Nigeria's fortified presidential complex in Abuja. For many Nigerians in the southwestern states, the convictions also signified a continued hostility by a northern regime toward Yoruba access to power, as shown in the violent May 1 demonstrations in Ibadan after the announcement of the convictions.

These developments raise questions about the interests and motives of different groups within the military. As a western diplomat remarked to our mission, "Since the 1980s many people have joined the army as a means to political power." Close observers of the Nigerian military have also noted that many of the more "professional" officers were forced out by the Abacha regime. Additionally, there is strong evidence that Yorubas and other non-northern groups have been culled from the officer corps, particularly in view of the December 1997 arrests.[9] Such actions indicate a set of crosscurrents within the military leadership that add to the uncertainty surrounding this pivotal institution. While the Nigerian military remains generally opaque to outsiders, there are indications that some officers would like to see a withdrawal from politics and a return to more professional functions. A number of retired senior officers have informally urged the permanent extrication of the military from politics. However, the military has not declared an institutional commitment to return to the barracks. Many officers and enlisted personnel are evidently motivated by sectional or purely venal concerns.

In light of these uncertainties, the selection of Major General Abdulsalam Abubakar as head of state following General Abacha's death on June 8, 1998, can be taken as a hopeful development. As chief of defense staff, General Abubakar was essentially next in line for succession, especially since Abacha's deputy, General Diya, had been arrested and sentenced to death for plotting a coup. The prompt decision of the Provisional Ruling Council, the military committee that convened after Abacha's death, indicated some regard for official procedure and the chain of command. In addition, General Abubakar, a Muslim from the middle belt, has a reputation for professionalism and a lack of apparent political aspirations. There is some early promise that he might align with moderates within the military, who are amenable to political reform, and resist hard-liners pressing for continued authoritarian rule.

A further issue is the lack of a clear compact, or even substantive dialogue, between civilian and military elites. Since Nigeria's first coup d'état in 1966, military leaders have regularly stated a preference for democracy as a "normal" political condition, and they have promised a rapid return to the barracks. Yet Nigeria has witnessed six successful military interventions, and officers have ruled the country for all but ten years since independence in 1960 (see Table 3.2). The quest for a professionalized armed forces has been offset by the stubborn reality of chronic cycles of civil and military rule. When civilians have governed, during the Second Republic (1979–83) and briefly in 1993, it has been at the discretion of the military. There has not been direct public discussion, or an organizational arrangement, to secure a stable equilibrium between civil and military institutions.

Abacha's military-led transition to supposedly civilian rule was essentially compromised by the lack of a clear counterweight to military authority. In the absence of a constitution, there was no formal arrangement for the assertion of civilian control over government. The 1995 constitution, even if implemented, may contain inherent flaws that will limit its effectiveness. A prominent Nigerian lawyer said, "The last two constitutions [of 1989 and 1995] are self-imposed agendas of the military." Moreover, the Abacha regime refused an open dialogue with civilian political forces. General Abacha's speech on October 1 (Independence Day), 1997, admonished his critics to relent and join the regime's official transition program; he conceded no legitimate role for the opposition and did not offer any opening for discussion with dissident forces. This blunt attitude reflected the regime's stance since seizing power. The planned shift from military rule hinged mainly upon the promises of General Abacha and his close associates. This premise was inherently fragile and susceptible to reversal, as seen in the steps toward Abacha's self-succession in the final months of his rule.

THE DILEMMA OF PLURAL IDENTITIES: DIVERSITY AND CENTRALIZATION

Nigeria is an amalgamation of diverse precolonial societies, states, and cultures. This diversity has fostered challenges to the country's development and stability, a problem closely linked to the economic role of the state. Among the most striking themes in Nigeria's postindependence history has been the tension between a plural society pressing for autonomy and distributive fairness and a state that has increasingly concentrated political and economic power in itself and the elites that control it. Both long-term structural dilemmas and more immediate difficulties arise from the recent political crisis. Nigeria attained independence in 1960 as a "geographic expression" in the words of an eminent nationalist figure.[10] The colonial boundaries encompassed some 250 linguistic groups, myriad ethnic and religious identities, and several broad regional distinctions. A crucial dimension of political life has been the contention among ethnic, regional, and religious groups.[11]

A perennial challenge in the ensuing decades has been the search for an effective formula to integrate the distinct cultural, economic, and political demands of this heterogeneous society. The costs of division were powerfully demonstrated in the bitter civil war of 1967–70, which claimed perhaps two million lives. Since that time, Nigerian governments have invoked the need for the constitutional and fiscal mechanisms of a workable federalism, and several regimes have sought to craft such arrangements. This process has evolved in the context of a mixed economy with a considerable role for private enterprise.

Although the principles of federalism suggest a need for power sharing and a dispersal of opportunities, the combination of oil income and military rule has fostered a concentration of authority and resources. Over the past thirty years, Nigeria has been governed by a succession of military regimes, with a brief civilian hiatus during the Second Republic. During the same period, the influx of abundant revenues from petroleum exports has encouraged fiscal centralization and a large government role in the economy. Consequently, a rentier state has evolved mainly under authoritarian control. Control of the state has also been skewed toward northern ethnic and regional groups.

Military and civilian governments alike have responded to sectional pressures with strategies combining selective largesse for some and coercion for others. Distributive politics in Nigeria have been defined formally through constitutional apportionments, the creation of states, and changing revenue allocation formulas. The actual politics of distributing oil revenues, however, has undermined these institutions, as leaders have used the informal mechanisms of patron-client relations and illicit practices to direct resources to friends and followers. When such inducements have proved insufficient for political control, leaders have turned to political repression or armed force.

These tactics have been successful in securing particular regimes and preserving a measure of political cohesion in a potentially fractious setting. Yet the politics of distribution have also created liabilities for the country's long-term development. This approach to political management fosters prodigious corruption, depleting resources and undermining economic growth. One leading writer on Nigeria's political economy has described it as a "prebendal" system, in which public resources are widely diverted for private ends.[12] In these circumstances, state revenues and programs have been captured by numerous claimants, either on behalf of particular communities and interests or for purely personal gain. In consequence, governments lack the independence and stability to pursue long-term development, while groups in civil society focus on extracting patronage rather than pursuing growth-enhancing investments. Prebendal politics have been divisive because patronage tends to work along ethnic and regional lines, encouraging competition and mistrust among groups. Moreover, distributive politics have been highly inequitable. While elites have benefited from the extravagant gains of the oil economy, most popular strata and even segments of the middle class have felt insecure and excluded.[13]

For all these reasons, the patronage system has been inherently unstable. Since material inducements offer the main source of political allegiance, governments are vulnerable to a loss of resources, and fluctuations in oil revenues have had unsettling effects. The centralized control of resources and government intervention in the economy has raised the stakes of political office, creating intense competition for access to power. The result has been a cycle of instability and decline, as struggles over resources have displaced regimes and political uncertainty has undermined economic growth. The interplay of intense ethnic and regional conflicts with a centralized, distributive state forms the core of the Nigerian dilemma.

THE DIMENSIONS OF COMMUNAL COMPETITION

The pivotal communal conflicts include those among the three region-ally dominant groups—southwestern Yoruba, southeastern Igbo, and northern Hausa-Fulani. These rivalries are mingled with the influence of sundry ethnic minorities. The central middle belt of the country is a diverse zone of transition between north and south and often acts as a political balance. Various minorities have contended with dominant groups, other minorities, and the state. While the original regional divi-sions continue as a salient dimension of ethnic rivalry, the politics of communalism in Nigeria have become more complex and varied in the decades since independence.

Competition among these groups has taken on new aspects with the rise of the oil economy. At independence, each region had a distinctive cash crop economy, led in the west by cocoa, in the east by palm pro-duce, and in the north by groundnuts and cotton. The ethnically dom-inated regional governments had discretion over their separate export revenues, affording a degree of autonomy to different groups. Petroleum assets, however, are heavily concentrated in the southeast, while the commercial and financial activities the oil revenue generates have grown substantially in the southwest. More important than the location of resources, however, is the monopolization of oil revenue by the federal government. Northern elites have access to this wealth through con-trol of the central state, and they consequently fear that diminution of their political leverage will leave them at an economic disadvantage. Southern groups, who are better situated in the private economy, resent their perceived marginalization in the political system.

Another broad fissure, encompassing both religion and ethnicity, has been evident between the northern and southern portions of the country. The north is overwhelmingly Muslim and is dominated by a relatively cohesive elite, owing to the historical legacy of the emirate system and the Borno empire. The south is more diverse in both eth-nicity and religion and has a correspondingly more disparate leader-ship. The Igbo and the southeastern minorities are almost entirely Christian. The Yoruba are nearly equally divided among Christians and Muslims, with very little internal religious conflict. At the national level, however, an explicit division between Christian and Muslim reli-gious communities has animated politics in recent years. This division has been incited by a number of issues, including the government takeover of mission schools in 1976, the establishment of shari'a courts in the 1979 constitution, Nigeria's membership in the Organization of the Islamic Conference since 1985, the government subsidy for Muslim pilgrims to Mecca, the access to government of peak associations from different religious communities, and the growing concern and tension surrounding local outbursts of religious violence. In some circumstances the sectional division between north and south has been expressed through religious discourse.

These communal divisions are not monolithic. There are currents and segments among each of these general groupings. Diversity gives rise to a complex and shifting set of alliances and antipathies. Nonetheless, certain lines of cleavage have featured in the country's leading political crises, as they have in the current situation. Since independence, the central government has been substantially dominated by groups associated with a broad, northern Muslim establishment. Southern ethno-regional groups have perceived a political hegemony by the north, although at times they have entered into expedient alliances with northern political forces, especially against each other. As we noted in the preceding historical overview, eastern elites have periodically formed coalitions with northern parties, although these have not been durable. The civil war, however, pitted the Igbo community against the federal government in a conflict that drew northern and Yoruba groups together against the Biafran secession. A lasting antipathy between Igbo and Yoruba communities has been evident since that struggle. The legacy of north-south strife is reflected in the friction between the northern-dominated government and communities in the southwest and the Niger Delta. A degree of informal ethnic balancing has been reflected in the participation of numerous southern politicians in the cabinet and the transition program, but the events surrounding the alleged coup plot in December 1997 indicate the depth of Yoruba alienation from the present regime, that regime's suspicion of Yoruba elites, or both.

Divisions within northern Nigeria have also been important. These are expressed through elite factions, which represent different local alliances, economic interests, traditional status distinctions, and sometimes religious preferences. There is also a recurrent tension between elites and grassroots movements, some of which carry on the populist tradition of Aminu Kano (see Chapter 2), others of which represent more radical strands of Islam. The elite divisions in the north have been manifest in General Abacha's removal in March 1996 of Ibrahim Dasuki as the sultan of Sokoto and in an intraregional shift of appointments and influence. The Dasuki episode resonates widely in the north. Dasuki was installed as sultan of Sokoto in 1988 with the support of General Babangida. The sultan of Sokoto is the most prestigious emirate title, and the incumbent of the position is also invited to become president of the Supreme Council of Islamic Affairs, in effect the public leader of Nigerian Muslims. A well-known businessman and politician, Dasuki was viewed in many quarters as an illegitimate arriviste who had usurped the position from Mohammed Maccido, the "rightful" hereditary sultan. There was considerable gratification in Sokoto when Abacha deposed and arrested Dasuki in March 1996. Dasuki was charged with violations of banking laws and was banished from Sokoto, under house arrest in shifting locations, until his release in June 1998.[14] Abacha's intervention was commonly viewed as a repudiation of Babangida's authority as well as an assertion of power over the Sokoto elite. A Kano native from a Kanuri background, Abacha altered the traditional alliance between the Hausa-Fulani elites in Kano and Sokoto, introducing a stronger linkage between Kano and the Kanuri power center of Borno. This implied an incipient power shift within the north.

Some other elements of communal competition are noteworthy in the current situation. The lasting tension between Igbo and Yoruba political elites has discouraged a broad alliance of southern groups. In addition, northern progressive elements who had allied with Chief Abiola's party in the 1993 elections have become estranged from the Abiola camp, reacting to what they view as the sectional nature of partisan appeals following the annulment. As one northern prodemocracy figure observed, "The problem of sectionalism has made [the democracy movement] difficult to continue [in the north]" because many northerners view the June 12 cause as a "Yoruba" issue. The virtual collapse of the official transition program after the five-party nomination of Abacha and the low turnout in the April 1998 elections, raised the possibility that a national democratic consensus could be revived. The new political situation in the wake of Abacha's death makes that prospect more urgent.

In one sense, the Abacha regime deployed the traditional Nigerian skills of ethnic statecraft. Leaders used public appointments, administrative divisions, constitutional changes, and informal patronage to effect, bringing a diverse array of groups into tacit acceptance of the regime. There has nonetheless been a distinct northern bias in senior-level appointments by the government. Repression has also been an adjunct to patronage, as the military has been uncompromising in quelling challenges from opposition groups.

Yet there have been evident limitations to this strategy. The general weakness of the Nigerian economy and the continued dependence of state revenues on petroleum creates an inherent constraint on patronage resources especially at a time of falling oil prices. Without a dramatic expansion of growth and economic diversification, government largesse will be restricted. Moreover, the strategy of ad hoc distribution (and accompanying coercion) fails to alleviate the lingering resentment and divisiveness carried over from the June 12 crisis.

THE PROBLEM OF INCLUSION: YORUBA DISAFFECTION

The aftermath of the June 1993 election, in which a Yoruba candidate was prevented from taking office by a predominantly northern regime, has left deep resentment among much of the western heartland. Supporters of democracy from diverse regions and ethnic groups opposed the annulment of the elections, but Yorubas experienced a specific feeling of disfranchisement. The nation's important centers of commerce, intellectual life, and (for most of its postindependence history) the political capital were located in their territory, and they have commonly dominated the country's civil society and democratic movements. Other ethnic groups, in particular from the north and middle belt, relied more heavily on the military and the public service for social mobility. Feelings of disfranchisement in the Yoruba region are intensified by memories of electoral fraud and political exclusion in the crises of 1962–66, and again in the 1983 elections. Many Yorubas perceive a systematic effort by northern elites to block them from power at the national level, and they maintain that the prospect of a western president caused military leaders to side against the 1993 transition.

The delegation heard this view repeatedly in its discussions in Lagos and Ibadan. Such opinions are not entirely without foundation. A northern intellectual recounted for us the widespread opposition among the northern elite toward ceding power to southerners. He commented that this group was concerned that Yorubas would use political power to bolster their dominant position in the economy, leaving the north as virtual "slaves." Many in the southwest are aware of these sentiments; the continuing impasse over June 12 and such provocations as the "Yoruba Agenda" pamphlet are regarded as further signs of their political isolation. We have also seen that southerners often use similar language in lamenting the oppressive "northern yoke" maintained by a shadowy "Kaduna Mafia" of northern notables. Whatever the basis of these mutual images, the development of hostile stereotypes of different ethno-regional groups is a fundamental challenge to Nigerian unity.

Frustrations among many Yorubas have inspired a latent and at times explicit desire for political detachment from the north. For instance, even such a prominent establishment figure as Oba Moses Adetona Daisi of Odogbolu reacted to the arrests of Yoruba alleged coup plotters in December 1997 by saying, "It is an incident that can determine the unity of Nigeria."[15] Daisi is the traditional ruler of the hometown of General Oladipo Diya, who was charged with leading the plot. Such emotions, though often dormant, pose an implicit threat to Nigeria's federal compact. Since the 1993 election crisis, repeated episodes of civil violence have racked the southwestern states. Some observers have suggested that the string of antimilitary bombings in Lagos also displays this regional frustration, although it must be stressed that the government has produced no evidence indicating the source of the attacks. Not all violence in the Yoruba areas has been directed against the government. Beginning in May 1997, a recurrent conflict between the Ife and Modakeke communities erupted once again following the relocation of a local government headquarters, and as many as three hundred killings were reported over a period of several months. This dispute has a lineage going back to the nineteenth century, but it is significant that recent outbursts have occurred in periods of political tension, notably during the 1983 elections in the Second Republic.[16]

THE SOUTHERN MINORITIES

These tensions are augmented by the continuing dispute between the government and Ogoni activists in the southeastern oil-producing region. The Movement for the Survival of the Ogoni People (MOSOP) has agitated for a greater allocation of revenues to the oil-producing areas, increased development assistance and employment opportunities in these communities, and more attention to the substantial environmental hazards arising from oil and gas production. The protests in Ogoniland have included direct action against Shell Oil (which suspended activities in the Ogoni areas in 1994) in addition to petitioning the Nigerian government. The government, concerned about the security of its most strategic economic activity, has responded with repression. A heavy state security presence in Ogoniland, persistent human rights abuses, and an absence of government dialogue with minority dissidents have furthered tensions in the Niger Delta states. Members of the working group have met with MOSOP representatives, oil company executives, the head of the government's development fund for the oil-producing regions, and recent visitors to the area.

Government security forces apparently operate in the oil-producing areas with impunity and are allegedly responsible for continuing human rights violations in Ogoniland. The Abacha regime maintained a hard line against MOSOP. While military rulers have sought to bring some traditional Ogoni leaders into a cooperative relationship with the government, they have bluntly suppressed dissidents in the region. Despite these actions, continuing tensions between local communities and foreign firms present an impediment to future investment in the petroleum sector.

The problems in Ogoniland have been compounded by growing tensions among other groups in the Niger Delta region. Beginning in early 1997, and escalating in the weeks after the March local government elections, violence erupted in several parts of the coastal oil-producing zones. Members of the Ijaw, Itsekiri, and Urhobo communities, embroiled in sporadic fighting throughout the region, targeted oil company facilities and personnel. Armed bands seized several flow stations, sabotaged equipment, and took a number of company employees hostage.[17] The immediate spark for the disturbances was an intercommunal dispute over the boundaries of local government areas and electoral districts, which were redrawn by the regime in October 1996. The conflict, however, spoke to deeper complaints about government neglect of the oil-producing areas, frustration over economic malaise and environmental degradation, and resentment over the confines of political representation for minority communities. This is another instance where government policies have aggravated rather than calmed conflict.

RELIGIOUS TENSION AND MOBILIZATION

Ethnicity is only one source of identity in Nigeria. In recent years, religious mobilization and interreligious tension have also become increasingly salient issues, a new dimension in Nigeria's turbulent history. In an environment of economic uncertainty, rising inequality, and political exclusion, increasing numbers of Nigerians in this devout society have turned to alternative religious groupings as an important coping strategy. In both northern and southern portions of the country we observed an expansion of religious activities, and we spoke with several representatives of mainstream religious groupings who described energetic efforts at proselytizing. In Lagos, Ibadan, and Kaduna, we saw abundant signs of independent churches, especially among the Pentecostals and other evangelical movements. In Kano and other northern cities there has been a proliferation of autonomous mosques, as well as the emergence of nonconformist Muslim denominations or sects.

These groups often serve the material as well as spiritual needs of their followers. They provide a sense of community and meaning, along with some social welfare roles. As one northern commentator observed, "People organize at the religious level because the secular state does not address their own fundamental issues." Many groups are inward looking, localized, and oriented toward personal salvation, but several—notably the Muslim Brothers—have adopted a dissident stance toward both established religious institutions and the government.

Religious mobilization has sometimes given rise to competition and strife. In recent years, there has been a series of local religious clashes, often with ethnic overtones. Since the late 1980s, Christian-Muslim violence has erupted in the northern cities of Kano, Zaria, Bauchi, and Kaduna, along with the towns of Kafanchan, Zangon-Kataf, and Tafawa Balewa. Several hundred deaths and many more casualties have resulted from these incidents. The causes of the episodes have varied, from Muslim resentment over aggressive Christian evangelization to perceived religious insults and from disputes over the proximity of religious schools to the control of abattoirs. Such altercations are often bound up with issues of land, community boundaries, or local inequalities.

The rising visibility of the northern Islamist movement led by Sheik Ibrahim Zakzaky is a striking expression of dissident social currents. The Ikhwan, or Muslim Brothers, have been popularly dubbed as Shi'ite, a designation that owes more to Zakzaky's early personal connections with Iran than to the actual beliefs of his followers. Based in Zaria and Kaduna, the movement has become a significant social and religious force in the northern states. Like previous radical expressions of Islam in Nigeria, the Muslim Brothers draw their main support from young people, chiefly Koranic students, who have been marginalized by economic adversity and political closure. They have established a network of mosques along with other facilities such as schools, radio stations, and economic ventures.

The Muslim Brothers pose different challenges for political and civil elites in Nigeria. Sheik Zakzaky's close association with Iran, where he spent time as a student, has aroused confrontation with the prevailing northern Muslim establishment, which has historically been closer to Saudi Arabia. In addition, the grassroots character of Zakzaky's movement taps into the tradition of northern populism championed by the late leader Aminu Kano. A close observer of northern politics told us in the city of Kano, "The Talakawa—the common people—are quite prepared to bring about change. Their main grudge with the political system is with the *ancien régime* in northern Nigeria." The expression of religious populism suggests a broader wellspring of frustration, which characterizes some Christian communities as well. Since 1995, there have been growing tensions between the Muslim Brothers and authorities in the northern states. Members of the movement have been involved in confrontations with government forces in Zaria, Kaduna, Katsina, and Kano, resulting in numerous deaths and more than a hundred arrests, including that of Sheik Zakzaky.

A prime question raised by these developments is whether they are mainly localized expressions of discontent and friction or indicators of incipient, large-scale conflict in Nigeria. While many of the incidents noted here are clearly parochial, they touch upon wider issues of ethnic competition, regional antipathy, and religious division. In a number of authoritarian societies, religious institutions have provided the political space, and sometimes the leadership, for political opposition movements. In Nigeria however, religious mobilization could seriously divide rather than unite the society. Hence mechanisms of interreligious cooperation are vital to any future democratic transformation.[18]

ECONOMIC STAGNATION

The challenges of communal competition and social conflict have been heightened by the economic malaise Nigeria has witnessed for several years. Since 1990, yearly economic growth has averaged only 1.6 percent. In 1993 and 1994 inflation approached triple digits, and the naira collapsed to a quarter of its 1992 value. Economic mismanagement worsened considerably during the latter part of Babangida's rule, and General Abacha's regime aggravated many of these problems. The economy plummeted as the government pursued a series of detrimental policies in a context of political uncertainty and rampant corruption. Most of the elements of economic reform introduced during Babangida's early years were discarded. Government spending ran out of control as enormous sums were diverted to off-budget accounts without any documentation or accountability. The government printed money to cover widening budget deficits, and the velocity of monetary growth fed inflation. Policies of financial reform and privatization were stalled, while the regime sharply curtailed repayment on $33 billion in external debt. The government was also delinquent in paying its foreign partners in petroleum production, and officials threatened unilaterally to amend the basic contracts governing the oil industry.

Some of these shortcomings, especially in the area of stated policy and macroeconomic management, have improved since 1995. Yet the economy continues to show the effects of slow growth, massive unemployment, dwindling production, and a general lack of investor confidence. A few areas—such as inflation, exchange rates, and fiscal balances—look increasingly favorable, but these are somewhat deceptive. Many stabilization measures have obscured or actually worsened basic economic problems. The government has balanced the budget and contained the money supply partly by withholding disbursements, including debt service and needed capital spending. The government is at least $17 billion in arrears on external debt payments because it has for several years repaid far less than the amount due to creditors. In 1996, however, a fortuitous rise in the world price for crude oil, increased domestic prices for gasoline, and a value-added tax fortified the budget. The value of the naira has held fairly steady since late 1994, but this mainly reflects a depressed demand for hard currency resulting from low purchasing power and a shortage of financial liquidity. Such conditions also reduce inflationary pressures. These are hardly indications of sound macroeconomic management but rather token improvements that mask the underlying deterioration of the economy. Growth hovered slightly higher than 2 percent annually in 1995 and 1996, well below the rate of population increase; there was little indication of dramatic improvement in 1997. Agricultural production has remained stagnant. Manufacturing has declined about 3 percent annually during the past five years, and the financial sector shows signs of collapse.

Since 1995 Nigeria's vital oil industry has experienced unprecedented difficulties that could erode the foundations of the national economy. Among the leading problems are the government's uneven payment of cash calls to joint venture partners and its failure to resolve nearly $1 billion in arrears to oil production firms. Moreover, central authorities have underfunded petroleum development activities in recent years, forcing companies to cut back employees and reduce production goals. This suggests disarray within key ministries, as well as a fiscal crisis in the central administration. In response to these problems, the petroleum minister has blamed foreign oil companies and recommended a unilateral alteration of the Memorandum of Understanding

(MOU), which regulates the terms of partnership in the oil industry. These developments, in tandem with the collapse of the domestic refineries and the recurrent violence in the Niger Delta region, have checked the progress of new investments and output in this crucial sector. At a time when Nigeria's proven oil and gas reserves have sharply increased, and large new investments in natural gas activities are poised to begin, the chronic mismanagement in this area is particularly detrimental.

CIVIC DISENGAGEMENT AND THE DECLINE OF INSTITUTIONS

The decline of public institutions is integrally related to the economic malaise that has overtaken Nigeria. The drift toward institutional decline reflects the combined effects of political instability, prodigious corruption, and prolonged economic stagnation. The steady deterioration of primary public functions throughout the country constitutes another dimension of state weakness and social disaffection. Large segments of the Nigerian public have ceased to expect government provision of social services, public utilities, infrastructure, security, or administration. Many groups have resorted to self-help measures through religious, community, or civic organizations. This dissociation of citizens from government evokes the decline of such ramshackle states as Zaire under Mobutu or Liberia under Samuel Doe. While Nigeria has clearly not yet reached those depths, the course of institutional deterioration provides worrisome signs of future decay.

Agencies of public administration have deteriorated under a number of pressures. As a result of government austerity measures, real wages have declined, and staffing has been reduced in much of the public sector. Political instability has aggravated this uncertainty, while recent governments have tinkered with institutions and reshuffled personnel. Military interference in the bureaucracy has undermined administrative autonomy and weakened further the performance of public enterprises. Irregular funding and policies have additionally demoralized public agencies. Routine bureaucratic and regulatory roles—including customs and immigration, revenue collection, financial regulation, and central banking operations— have been irregular and substandard.

The government of General Abacha claimed to have undertaken some initiatives to rationalize customs procedures and operations at the ports, although, as we have noted, business representatives have observed little change in their day-to-day operations. For instance, one Nigerian business leader commented, "Corruption always crops up [as an issue for business], especially at the ports. At one time there were fifty-two official agencies at the ports. The situation became so difficult that the government decided to reduce the number to about eight. But many found their way back, and after the recent bombings there are also new special units that will join." Rationalization efforts, moreover, have not compensated for the erosion of basic capacity in leading institutions, and many business groups in Nigeria view the reforms as cosmetic. Endemic corruption, ranging from petty to grand, taints most public interactions with state officials. These are perennial features of Nigerian life, but the scale and severity of the problem has clearly worsened in recent years.

These same troubles are evident in the administration of law and order. Police and security agencies have generally failed to curb a rising tide of violent crime, while at the same time citizens are subject to flagrant harassment and corruption. "There are such high levels of violence in this society. The legitimization of violence impacts on every level," said a civic activist to our group. Indeed, there are widespread allegations of direct police collusion with armed robbers in some of the country's major cities. Members of our group were robbed at a police checkpoint between the airport and the city of Lagos. An obvious indication of the subversion of the security apparatus has been the failure to uncover any suspects in a string of high-profile murders and attacks over the past three years. Moreover, an increasingly corrupt judiciary and an overcrowded prison system compound the problems of instilling order or adjudicating disputes.

The collapse of social services is one of the central aspects of government failure experienced by many Nigerians. The educational system has broken down in recent years as a result of funding shortages, salary arrears, and political disputes between government and teachers. The university system has suffered markedly from the government's repressive response to academic protests. Our visits to universities in Ibadan and Kano revealed the extent of this decay, which was much more advanced in Ibadan. The "southwestern" universities are the objects of particular suspicion, as bases of opposition to the regime. Facilities were in disrepair, and the bookstores were sparsely stocked. In the words of one professor at the University of Ibadan, "I can't give my own students a fifth of the education I received here." In the aftermath of a 1996 strike by faculty members, after which their union was suppressed and some expelled from their homes in the rain, he noted that "very many people are not teaching, and this is not a functioning university." While the proliferation of new states has led to the establishment of new universities, this professor argued that "the issue is not the number. The issue is, we do not have a single good university." Many Nigerians have simply withdrawn their children from school because of prohibitive fees or low standards, and more affluent families seek alternative schooling at home or abroad.

The public health system is also in an advanced state of decline, as hospitals are lacking in supplies and much of the medical profession has emigrated in recent years.

Utilities and infrastructure also show the effects of sustained neglect and mismanagement. The chronically erratic power supplies in Lagos are often absent for days at a stretch, as we saw during our stay, and petroleum supplies are interrupted by refinery breakdowns or distribution problems. Ironically, drivers, transportation companies, and airlines in this major oil-exporting country are all subject to recurring fuel shortages. From June to September 1997, much of the country was idled as domestic refineries operated at a fraction of capacity while bickering government ministries hindered the importation and delivery of fuel. The fuel crisis surfaced again in 1998. Many roads in the country are in disrepair, and the railways have virtually ceased to function. Recent investments through the government's Petroleum Trust Fund are directed toward some of these problems, although they have been surrounded by controversy since a lack of public disclosure obstructs transparency in the use of these monies. There is also some credence to the suggestion we heard in Lagos that spending on infrastructure has been regionally unbalanced. One of the glaring incongruities we observed was the relative opulence of Abuja, which has absorbed enormous spending in recent years, contrasted with the degradation of public facilities in Lagos and Ibadan.

Nigeria's economic and institutional decline has important political implications. Many civic organizations, notably labor, women's, professional, and business groups, have been adversely affected by scarce resources and declining membership. As a person involved in the social sector emphasized, educational deficits and crumbling facilities have weakened organizations and diverted the attention of many Nigerians to their own basic needs. The middle classes have been among those most harshly affected by the travails of the economy. This segment of Nigerian society might be expected to provide a source of democratic pressure, yet many have been distracted by the struggle for a livelihood. A substantial number of professionals have migrated to other countries. Urban workers, those in the informal sector, and many in rural communities have suffered great privation. Economic problems have contributed to ethnic and religious conflict in many areas. An activist in Lagos put it well: "There is a lack of social capital in Nigeria." This refers to the demoralizing effects of economic deterioration as well as the material struggles of citizens. It should also be noted that general scarcity raises the premium on access to political power, with potentially destabilizing influences on the conduct of electoral politics.

The widespread alienation of citizens from public institutions is a direct reaction to sustained authoritarianism as well as the degeneration of both the economy and state administration. Many social groups are noticeably retreating from civic life, turning instead toward parallel institutions and independent social mobilization. Self-help strategies take different forms among disparate communities. More affluent citizens have recourse to private provision of security, education, health, electricity, and economic services. Some have simply left the system by emigrating. Members of the middle class are commonly engaged in professional associations, mainstream religious institutions, and community or village organizations. For the urban poor and those in the rural areas organizational resources are more sparse, but civic and community groups, religious welfare services, and informal social networks are available.

In addition, informal economic activities—including trade, services, and craft production—provide a source of livelihood for many Nigerians. The turn to parallel markets has increased as people seek creative ways of coping with a moribund economy. The more "legitimate" forms of informal activity recognized above are commonly practiced by average Nigerians. Alongside these endeavors, some Nigerians have cultivated a growing realm of illicit activities, which also reflect disengagement from the formal economy. Smuggling, drug trafficking, money laundering, and commercial fraud have become epidemic in Nigeria. Certain of these ventures, notably the narcotics trade and the incidence of business scams (known as "419" after the Nigerian criminal code for fraud), have spilled over Nigeria's boundaries to attain global scope. These activities provide a critical source of sustenance for a few in Nigerian society. They also carry substantial costs in terms of crime, capital flight, and adverse effects on Nigeria's already poor international reputation.

Despite all these survival strategies, more and more Nigerians simply lack the means to cope. Reliable statistics are missing, but a leader of one Protestant church told us his own observations: "If I compare

1975 to today, maybe people came to the church to ask for assistance, maybe two or three people in three months. Today there are ten every Sunday. And they are the ones who have the courage—because they are desperate."

OPPORTUNITIES FOR CHANGE?

The authoritarian status quo in Nigeria does not offer a sound basis for future stability and development. Nigeria's past experiences with democratic (or at least civilian electoral) politics were also marked by corruption and ethnic competition, and the public seems almost as cynical about civilian politicians as military rulers. Nonetheless, as one Protestant leader declared, "The politicians have not had the opportunity to learn from their failures." Democracy is not only an end in itself but also ultimately the only system that could provide stable, legitimate governance to Nigeria. Especially when set against the manifest failure of decades of authoritarian domination, democratic rule holds out new opportunities to address Nigeria's problems of unruly diversity, state weakness, and stunted economic performance.

Democracy combined with genuine federalism promises greater representation and autonomy for Nigeria's many cultural and geographic constituencies. In order to fulfill this potential, however, a transition to democracy in Nigeria must be grounded in a legitimate process of participation and inclusion. Political reform should follow accepted international standards of accountability and civic freedoms.

An open arena of political contestation obviously poses both opportunities and hazards. Disparate groups can air their differences and seek to achieve national accord, but they can also give voice to dissonant goals or separatist tendencies. Military governments tend to react to such rhetoric with repression, using nationalist exhortation or draconian internal security measures. It is evident, however, that suppressing expressions of diversity is more likely to foment conflict over the long term. A prominent Nigerian religious leader put the matter cogently to us: "Is the absence of war peace?" Within a more liberal political setting, the demands of political competition can foster negotiation and accommodation among partisan forces, while constitutional federalism can encourage a stable balance of power. Public participation, electoral choice, and an open political arena can restore some of the legitimacy depleted by rulers in recent years. In short, democratic development offers the most viable route away from Nigeria's current impasse. The pressing issue for Nigeria is whether, and under what conditions, democracy might reasonably be attained in the near term.

THE POLITICAL TRANSITION PROGRAM

In light of these concerns, a vital question is the relationship, if any, between the Abacha regime's purported transition to civilian rule and the broader goals of democratization in Nigeria. Despite the inevitable changes in the aftermath of Abacha's rule, his political program set an agenda for almost three years, and it echoed many traits of Babangida's previous military-led transition. Examining the features and flaws of the discredited Abacha transition can help to impart lessons about the needed future direction for a legitimate democratization process.

From our discussions with an array of Nigerians, our observations during the study mission, and our reading of events in Nigeria during the time since then, we concluded that Abacha's transition program lacked basic integrity or legitimacy and could not provide the foundation for a viable democratization process. The program's design has been problematic in many areas, and it was not implemented in a consistent or thorough fashion. Government repression created an inhospitable setting for competitive politics. General Abacha's nomination by all official parties and the planned substitution of an uncontested referendum for a presidential election removed any doubt about the transition's ultimate purpose: to perpetuate rule by the same unaccountable elites.

The official transition agenda announced by Abacha in October 1995 was to conclude on October 1, 1998 (Nigeria's thirty-eighth anniversary of independence), with a handover from military rule to an elected civilian government. A formal schedule was set in motion, and the official agenda appeared to be headed for a conclusion in October 1998, although the program lacked any genuine democratic content.

The government insisted that it was committed to a timely transfer of power to civilian authorities, while the political opposition, especially those aligned with Chief Abiola and the "June 12 mandate," portrayed the program as merely another ploy to sustain military government. Many ordinary Nigerians we encountered seemed resigned or apathetic toward the political transition, viewing it as an elite sideshow with little public involvement. "The transition program is designed not to lead to democracy. The military is not in dialogue with civil society and the opposition," stressed a human rights activist.

In some authoritarian systems, even carefully controlled transitions can at times develop a momentum that escapes their creators, but the Abacha regime prevented this in Nigeria. During our trip, we met a few political hopefuls who articulated a vision for the country and a commitment to public service, while at the same time we saw abundant signs of venality and opportunism among many party backers. Among the Nigerian people, cynicism toward politics and a fatigue with the military's "permanent transition" contended with fears of being excluded from access to public resources. One woman activist engaged in grassroots development work described the struggle with the rank and file: "We do not believe in this transition. We know it is a ruse, but [our members] want to participate." While such feelings did not legitimize the official transition program, they might have lent it a degree of importance. Since that discussion, however, the extraordinarily low turnout for the various elections has indicated that the public concluded the program was a sham.

As we have discussed, the political context of the transition has been fundamentally flawed. The scope of political competition was sharply restricted; the top-down management of the process hindered popular engagement, and there have been harsh limits on political rights. "[The government] should be liberalizing as they move toward the transition date, but they are becoming more repressive," observed a human rights advocate to our group. The press has been constrained, and political detainees, including the apparent president-elect of 1993, remained in confinement throughout the transition. A constitutional framework was not set in place. Authorities rigidly controlled the activities of political parties, and there was no independent electoral commission. In this environment, such functions as voter education and independent election monitoring were virtually impossible or meaningless. These circumstances negate the validity of the transition process.

The procedural details of the transition posed additional problems. The government published a transition schedule and established the major institutions of the program, including an officially controlled electoral commission. The National Electoral Commission of Nigeria (NECON), chaired by Chief Sumner Dagogo-Jack, served as an instrument of government supervision of the political process rather than as an independent, neutral administrative agency. A draft constitution was submitted to government in 1995, but it has not so far been released, and Nigeria's entire political process has been premised on rumors about the contents of that document. In addition, five political parties were registered in October 1996, after a screening process that excluded groups associated with the opposition (see Table 3.1). The parties are the United Nigerian Congress Party (UNCP), the Democratic Party of Nigeria (DPN), the Congress for National Consensus (CNC), the National Center Party of Nigeria (NCPN), and the Grassroots Democratic Movement (GDM). None has established a clear identity in terms of programs or regional appeal. Throughout our discussions in Nigeria in early 1997, none of the politicians or analysts we spoke to could name all the political parties or describe them in any detail. The more acerbic critics of government refer to the parties as "five fingers of one leprous hand." We saw little evidence of political party activity in the southwestern areas of the country, although there were more conspicuous signs in the northern cities.

Party-based local government polls, representing the first step in the election agenda, were held on March 15, 1997. Although the mechanics of the polling were uneventful, the voter register was vastly inflated, and the government did not publish detailed results until months following the election.[19] Elections for the thirty-six state legislatures, convened on December 6, 1997, were marked throughout the country by sparse voter turnout, but once again there were few disturbances in the voting. On April 25, 1998, elections were conducted for the National Assembly. The polling was uneventful, especially since turnout appeared to be around 5 percent. These elections all returned decisive leads for the UNCP, a party whose leaders had openly called for General Abacha to stand for president. By the end of 1997, there had already been substantial slippage in the original transition schedule. The government postponed the gubernatorial elections to coincide with the presidential poll on August 1, 1998. Appendix E includes the official transition timetable and the actual progress as of June 1998.

Although the five government-sponsored political parties selected General Abacha as their "consensus" presidential nominee in April 1998, a number of questions persisted. The general did not signal his immediate acceptance of the nominations, leaving the political process in limbo. The National Electoral Commission raised the possibility that the August 1 elections might be transformed into a simple referendum on General Abacha's tenure, while existing law seemed to prohibit a serving member of the armed forces from standing for office. Uncertainty and conjecture swirled around the transition program in its final months.

If the regime undertook a more open and credible transition, even if a flawed one, the transfer to civilian rule might have set the stage for a process of political reconciliation and future democratic reform including the establishment of civilian control over the military. This could have represented a departure from past decades of unaccountable authoritarian domination. The transition maintaining General Abacha's power under a civilian guise, however, failed to allay basic grievances and alleviate problems of governance. Such a circumstance aggravated fissures in the political system, and left open the possibility of future strife.

PROSPECTS FOR ECONOMIC REFORM

Economic reform is another critical issue confronting Nigeria. There is a pressing need to revive growth and to restructure Nigeria's economy. Economic recovery clearly is important for improving popular welfare and reducing the stresses of privation and inequality. Diversification is necessary to reduce Nigeria's dependence on a single export commodity subject to uncontrollable price fluctuation. A reduced economic role for the state might also liberate substantial resources and entrepreneurial energies, allowing enhanced equity, faster growth, and a more balanced economy. While there are signs that the current regime seeks to improve economic performance, the actual indications of reform and the prospects for implementation remain equivocal.

The Abacha government announced measures to address some leading problems of economic management. In 1996 and 1997, there were significant improvements in such problematic areas as inflation, exchange controls, budgetary imbalances, and unrecorded spending. Formal restrictions on capital movements and foreign investment were also relaxed significantly, and in October 1996 senior leaders proposed an extensive new privatization initiative, which would include the enormous and strategic oil and gas sector. The authorities launched a series of highly publicized measures allegedly to clean up the shambles in the financial sector, impose accountability for government contracts, cut down corruption at the ports, overhaul the customs service, and reduce the prevalence of drug trafficking, money laundering, and commercial fraud. Most of these policies, however, fell far short of what was proposed.

As in the political realm, there have been mixed signals on economic reform as well. Despite considerable anticipation, the 1997 and 1998 budgets essentially provided a continuation of existing policies rather than a forceful agenda for change. Performance during 1997 was lackluster, and there were few indications of a significant departure in economic management or a broader setting for economic activity. Reform initiatives are hindered by the potent entrenched interests that have benefited from a corrupt rentier economy. Since the military rulers themselves have been among the most powerful of these interests, it is difficult to see how they can implement the needed reform. In the near term, change will also be restricted by institutional weakness and by the country's poor reputation among investors. If credibility is to be restored in international markets, it will be essential for the Nigerian government to fulfill promises of liberalization, to sustain stable macroeconomic management, and to improve the quality of bureaucracy and regulation.

Recent alterations in policy and management have been paralleled by a more open dialogue between the government and the private sector over the course of economic governance. The Nigerian Economic Summit, a convocation of senior government officials and business leaders, has become an annual event bringing private sector representatives together with the policy establishment. The summit process prompted an even more ambitious program, Vision 2010, a forum to discuss the nation's future development. Involving two hundred invited participants for several months of exchange and debate, Vision 2010 included a significant cross section of Nigerian elites. After a series of seminars, the final report of the Vision 2010 committee was submitted to the government in October 1997. This process was modeled on a program in Malaysia, where it sparked a national debate. In Malaysia, however, despite some restriction on political debate (especially on sensitive ethnic issues), the process took place in the context of a representative government with some independent media. Participants in Malaysia's Vision 2020 process actually represented constituencies, and the meeting could prompt a national debate. In Nigeria's more authoritarian context, open public debate has largely been precluded, and the deliberations were limited to the vetted delegates at the meetings.

These events represent circumscribed, if significant, efforts to gather a constituency for economic change. Mindful once again of the restrictions on this government-sponsored process, there is still some latitude for interchange over basic aspects of the economy and political life. The Vision 2010 forum has encouraged discussion on basic features of development strategy, economic policy, and public institutions. In a seminar attended by study group members in early 1997, participants forcefully and candidly expressed the need for improved governance and more open politics as a basis for economic regeneration. Government sponsorship of these forums clearly limits their range of discussion, and many Nigerians we spoke to expressed indifference or hostility to this "stage-managed" process of dialogue. Nonetheless, some in the business community, and even some critics of government, welcomed the effort to air fundamental questions about Nigeria's economic future. As several participants acknowledged, the key test of the Vision 2010 process will be its implementation, over which the committee has no authority.

Change in the economic realm will ultimately depend on a credible transition to democratic rule. Only an accountable and legitimate government can begin to stabilize expectations and restore credibility to Nigeria's battered economy. At the same time, economic revival can provide a more solid basis for political reform. "The evolution of the economy will bring the rule of law into focus, because a strong economy requires the rule of law," noted a legal expert in speaking to our group. Having mismanaged and despoiled the economy for years, there is little reason to expect that Nigeria's military rulers have the capacity to engineer an economic recovery. The reform of Nigeria's economy is integrally related to a decisive improvement in governance.

PRESSURES FROM CIVIL SOCIETY

Apart from the measures taken by government leaders, there are other groups and mechanisms that can move Nigeria along a path of reform. The eclectic arena of civil society is an important yet neglected force. Within the nongovernmental realm there are numerous initiatives and activities that could advance an agenda of liberalization. The activities of nonpartisan groups dedicated to human rights and the rule of law are most prominent. These are aided in varying degrees by academics, professionals, women, and organized labor. Voices from the business community have increasingly pressed for improved governance as a necessary foundation for economic recovery. Some of the major religious denominations have also advocated greater openness in political life. Although the nongovernmental sector has been working under considerable duress, it remains a continuing source of dialogue, dissent, and participation. Civil society is the leading stimulus for democratic change.

The role of nongovernmental institutions in fostering domestic conflict resolution has frequently been overlooked. In Nigeria's hazardous political landscape, struggles between government and opposition have the potential to spiral into broader turmoil. It is important to limit the unintended and unmanageable consequences of political dissension. Nigeria's civil society embraces a number of "shock absorbers" that can alleviate or subdue social conflict. These include eminent members of the Muslim and Christian establishments, grassroots organizations within the different religious communities, civic organizations involved in monitoring conflict and developing peacemaking techniques, and circles of scholars and professionals from diverse backgrounds. These elements can serve as buffers and intermediaries between ethnic, religious, or partisan forces, and they may provide a set of honest brokers in national political dialogue. We examine these questions in fuller detail in the next chapter.

— 5 —

THE ROLE OF CIVIL SOCIETY

While in the short run civil society in Nigeria is constrained by repression and military rule, as well as chronic shortages of resources, in the long run its support is essential to the foundation of a self-governing society and a more accountable state. Indeed, despite the closure of political space, in recent years civic organizations have been among the most tenacious advocates of democratic aims. An active, diverse, and capable civil society can be crucial in assuring government accountability, creating a vibrant arena of public debate and political competition, shifting politics away from personal and ethnic appeals and toward a focus on issues or programs, encouraging the inclusion of diverse social groups, and safeguarding the legitimacy of new institutions. In addition to providing a bridge between government and the public, between state and society, intermediate associations can foster dialogue and accommodation among different communities. In the quest for stability and durable power sharing among elements of a plural society, civic groups can play indispensable roles. During our many conversations in Nigeria, a member of a grassroots women's organization working on health and development, among other issues, expressed the groups' mission especially well: "This is political work. We are building the capacities of people to participate in the structures of this society." Therefore, we believe that, even as international forces press the military to exit from power, as we argue they should, it is also vital to offer support for those domestic groups that can encourage a sustainable and legitimate basis for democratic politics.

A wide spectrum of societal organizations continues to function in Nigeria, although these groups face substantial limitations at present. Political repression and a depressed economy pose the most obvious challenges to independent associations, but a variety of organizational problems also hinder their scope and effectiveness. The leadership of many groups is dominated by middle-class professionals, although a few civic organizations have been able to mobilize larger constituencies for public action. Many associations are also isolated by narrow regional or ethnic membership. The problems of cultivating a broad political base have been aggravated by the general estrangement between civic organizations and civilian political elites. In addition, the diverse strands of civil society have not yet generated effective common strategies or programs. The authoritarian regime, with its destruction of any open national political space and restrictions on freedom of expression and association, has made it extremely difficult to address these problems.

For foreign groups and individuals preoccupied with governance, human rights, and stability in Nigeria, engagement with civil society is an important though sometimes neglected element of strategy. In surveying the array of nongovernmental organizations in Nigeria and the diverse international groups with concerns in the country, we have identified several clusters of common interest and association. These affiliations create the basis for strengthening networks among Nigerians as well as between Nigerians and potential partners outside the country. The clusters can usefully be identified with six categories: democracy and human rights, popular associations, conflict resolution, media, religion, and business. This section offers a description of the constituent groups and general conditions associated with each category, including possible avenues for international collaboration.

DEMOCRACY, HUMAN RIGHTS, AND LAW

Organizations dedicated to democratic reform, human rights, and the rule of law have been in the vanguard of efforts to resist authoritarianism in Nigeria. Several groups in this area have demonstrated impressive capacities in the face of difficult constraints, and they have played a number of important roles. These organizations have been actively involved in protesting abuses by government, chronicling violations, disseminating information, and adopting the cases of those persecuted by the regime. Many of their members have in turn suffered imprisonment and persecution themselves. In addition, this professional community has a special function in debating judicial or constitutional change and prescribing key political reforms. These activists and professionals can raise independent, critical voices regarding the legal and institutional features of the transition process.

Consequently, this segment of civil society can be instrumental in improving the immediate political environment, as well as influencing the features of an eventual democratic regime.

HUMAN RIGHTS AND DEMOCRACY ORGANIZATIONS

Several major organizations are committed to the advocacy of democratic rule, while a number of allied groups are engaged in non-partisan work on human rights and the rule of law. Leading prodemocracy organizations include the National Democratic Coalition (NADECO), the Campaign for Democracy (CD), Democratic Alternative (DA—a 1994 offshoot of CD), Community Action for Popular Participation (CAPP), and the National Conscience Party. The CD is relatively dormant at present, and other leading groups such as NADECO have experienced state repression. The United Democratic Front of Nigeria (UDFN), an aggregation of thirteen groups formed in 1996, has been more visible internationally than domestically. In May 1997 a group of twenty-two domestic human rights and civic associations in Nigeria announced the formation of a new coalition, United Action for Democracy (UAD), that would seek to promote democratic processes and values and, more specifically, resist any plan for self-succession by General Abacha. In April 1998, elements of UAD joined Gani Fawehinmi and other prodemocracy groups in the 40-member Joint Action Committee of Nigeria (JACON). This domestic organization mirrored a coalition of prodemocracy groups in exile, known as the Joint Action Committee, or JACOM.

In the area of human rights, several organizations have focused on general legal issues and specific judicial cases. Principal groups include the Constitutional Rights Project (CRP), the Civil Liberties Organization (CLO), and the Committee for the Defense of Human Rights (CDHR). Some human rights advocates have been affiliated with the Campaign for Democracy, the UAD, and JACON, and have generally supported democratization, albeit without commitment to a particular candidate or party.

Human rights and democracy groups have operated under severe constraints, notably the detention of their members, interference with foreign travel, public vilification by government, surveillance by security agencies, and the obstruction of their legal efforts. Most of these groups are based in Lagos or other southern cities, with a constituency mainly among middle-class professionals. Several, however, have sought to establish nationwide networks. These efforts should be supported.

THE LEGAL PROFESSION

Aside from the community of human rights activists, mainstream legal practitioners also have an interest in the general rule of law, and many lawyers have individually adopted political or human rights cases. The National Association of Democratic Lawyers (NADL) has been the most activist organization in the profession. The Nigerian Bar Association (NBA) has traditionally represented a diverse constituency, embracing members with a political agenda alongside a large population with narrower professional concerns. At present, the NBA is effectively split in two, in the wake of a factional dispute aggravated (if not provoked) by government interference in an internal election. One section represents dissident elements who have adopted a stance critical of government, in support of rapid democratization and improved legal standards. The "official" NBA embodies a more conservative outlook, in accord with basic government positions. The division of the NBA has significantly blunted its impact.

RECOMMENDATIONS

International organizations should place first priority on defending these groups and individuals from government repression and second priority on supporting their activities, especially those aimed at building wider national and international networks. While many outside groups prefer to remain neutral on specific partisan demands, there should be strong support for campaigns in the areas of human rights and the rule of law. This entails consistent pressure on the Nigerian regime to respect political rights and allow due legal process. Governments and external groups must protest loudly and promptly when activists are harassed and detained, defendants are sentenced without proper procedure, or the regime abrogates judicial independence by decrees and other interventions. Release of such detainees and full freedom for these organizations to pursue their work must be a key condition for acceptance of any transition program.

Beyond this basic concern, there are other actions that can strengthen efforts in these areas. Nigerian organizations can benefit from additional resources, both financial and organizational. In recent years, funding for such groups has been insufficient, and even those resources that have been approved have often not been disbursed. International donors should promptly issue adequate funds to support these associations—an admonition that applies for aid to civil society in general. Assistance with communications, such as desktop publishing and Internet capability, would be especially important.

More essential, however, are efforts to support Nigerian NGOs in their efforts to strengthen domestic networks and develop international linkages. Perhaps the most immediate problem within the human rights community, aside from state repression, is the relative isolation of groups and the dissipation of their efforts. This point was repeatedly stressed during the study group's visit to Nigeria. The leader of one organization in Lagos, discussing their principal challenges, told us candidly: "Many NGOs are concerned only with their own programs. Networking is lacking. Some . . . do not have the capacity to reach out to other parts of the country." The head of a grassroots women's organization also spoke of the need to expand training and political education throughout the country. An important goal is "trying to link the local to the national and international arena." Foreigners can address these needs by sponsoring meetings and seminars among Nigerian NGOs, either within the country, in other African states (whether within the subregion or in southern Africa), or outside of Africa entirely. International organizations and NGOs can increase their outreach toward groups in Nigeria and support Nigerian involvement in international meetings and forums. These efforts should be assisted by major foundations and counterpart NGOs abroad, as well as official sources like the U.S. Information Agency, USAID, the British Council, and appropriate United Nations agencies.

POPULAR AND PROFESSIONAL ASSOCIATIONS

The groups we include under the heading of "popular associations" constitute the broadest segment of civic life, encompassing dozens of organizations in many different areas of interest. We note the major groupings here, while Appendix C offers a more complete listing. Despite their varied concerns and activities, it is possible to generalize about this realm of associations. The popular strands of civil society play important roles in advancing public dialogue and pressing the government to address the needs of Nigerian citizens. By representing their diverse constituencies, these groups introduce genuine issues into politics, including health, education, the status of women, environmental protection, economic growth, equity, and social welfare. Nigerian politicians and military leaders alike often ignore these issues in favor of patronage politics and self-aggrandizement. Civic associations also frequently support general demands for the rights of free speech and assembly, better standards of governance, and economic development. Consequently, popular associations are essential to linking people with government, incorporating neglected groups such as women, students, ethnic minorities, and the poor, overcoming regional divisions, and ensuring wide representation in politics.

Labor Unions

Organized labor has historically been among the strongest elements of civil society. For this reason, military governments have targeted the labor movement to make it one of the most tightly controlled areas of mass organization. The Abacha regime took steps to neutralize the independent leadership of major labor groups and to shift away from a national model of organization toward a decentralized pattern of local or shop unions.

Since the late 1980s, government intervention in the peak labor confederation, the Nigerian Labour Congress (NLC), has undermined the organization's autonomy and ensured a quiescent leadership. The NLC has been diffident throughout the recent political crisis and is currently under the control of a government-appointed administrator. While individual unions within the NLC continue to work on mainstream economic issues, the union movement has been forced to abandon political engagement. The disposition of particular unions toward the authorities still varies by region and sector, with some industries and local affiliates taking a more assertive stance, though most have proved compliant in the face of repression.

The two petroleum sector unions, the National Union of Petroleum and Natural Gas Employees (NUPENG) and the Petroleum and Natural Gas Senior Staff Association (PENGASSAN), are now inactive. Their senior leaders, first among them NUPENG head Frank Kokori and PENGASSAN chief Milton Dabibi, were imprisoned after the politically motivated oil strikes of 1994 and released only in June 1998. Government administrators assumed control of union affairs. These unions have been closely monitored by state security agencies, and their finances are tightly regulated.

Women's Organizations

These include a broad range of groups, from the government-controlled National Council of Women's Societies (NCWS) and the officially accepted Federation of Muslim Women's Associations of Nigeria

(FOMWAN) to independent membership organizations such as Women in Nigeria (WIN) and smaller projects like the Empowerment and Action Research Center (EMPARC). In addition, numerous small-scale groups, some with no more than a few members, are active on specific issues such as women's health, child welfare, legal issues, AIDS education, and other concerns.

Many of these independent organizations experience little direct interference from government, especially when their programs deal with health, education, or other areas not deemed politically sensitive. Still, a person active in social sector work commented to our study group that "nothing is easy to do today in Nigeria, even in 'easy' areas like health." Some groups have been openly critical of the military regime and have suffered from state retaliation. Declining social conditions have intensified demands on the scarce resources of many grassroots organizations. A few social service organizations have found themselves in unexpected "competition" with the former first lady, Maryam Abacha, who sought to cultivate an image as a benefactor to Nigerian women and children. In at least one instance, as recounted by a donor representative, a Nigerian involved in antihunger activities was detained after winning a foreign award for work that paralleled the first lady's official program.

Students and Academics

The National Association of Nigerian Students (NANS) has been among the most militant civic organizations in Nigeria over the past decade. NANS has been involved in recurrent protests over poor educational standards, inadequate government funding for the university system, and student concerns on particular campuses. The association also played an important role in several demonstrations in the 1993-94 crisis period, in which a number of students died. An unknown number of students were among the more than one hundred people killed during disturbances in Lagos and Ibadan in the aftermath of the 1993 election annulment, and four students at the University of Benin were killed by police during protests in August 1994, following the arrest of Chief M. K. O. Abiola. Since that time, NANS leaders have been arrested or harassed, and the organization has been less visible as a political force. The government banned NANS nationally along with the Academic Staff Union of Universities (ASUU), the Non-Academic Staff Union of Universities (NASU), and the Senior Staff Association of Nigerian Universities (SSANU) in May 1996.[1]

ASUU, representing faculty, has consistently played an activist role, mingling protests over declining educational conditions with political challenges to the government. A protracted strike on university campuses in 1996 ended with the firing or resignation of hundreds of academic staff, along with a full government proscription of all ASUU activities in August. The government wants to replace the national organization with individual staff associations on university campuses. While this has been resisted by some leading ASUU members, no organization (official or nonofficial) is presently available to faculty at Nigerian universities.

ENVIRONMENTAL GROUPS

Nigeria does not have a strong domestic environmental movement, although several local associations have addressed specific problems. The most visible organization active in this area has been the Movement for the Survival of the Ogoni People (MOSOP), which represents local development and social equity concerns as well as problems of the environment in the ethnic Ogoni areas. Alongside the Ogoni and other community activists in the Niger Delta region, the Environmental Rights Action project of the Civil Liberties Organization has focused explicitly on these concerns. International groups such as Greenpeace and the Sierra Club have also raised general problems of erosion, deforestation, toxic dumping, and pollution, as well as degradation in the oil-producing areas. They are concerned with the framework for regulation, the technical problems of perceiving environmental quality, and the representation of local communities facing ecological difficulties. The government's repressive stance toward the Ogoni movement has had effects on environmental issues generally. Because many of these problems are associated with both the oil industry and ethnic claims of autonomy and control over resources, the regime has treated activism in this area as a national security threat. General Abacha referred to activists in the delta as "unpatriotic" in an October 1, 1997, speech.

THE MEDICAL PROFESSION

The Nigerian Medical Association (NMA) has a history of political activism extending back several years. Past protests by the association over professional working conditions and government funding for health services have escalated into confrontations with previous regimes. In addition, the National Association of Nigerian Nurses and

Midwives (NANNM) and the Medical and Health Workers Union of Nigeria (MHWUN) have represented the interests of other health professionals. The latter organization has been more politically active. The NMA has not been prominent in recent political controversies, owing mainly to government persecution of its most dissident members and the large-scale emigration of medical professionals in recent years.

LOCAL AND ETHNIC ASSOCIATIONS

Nigerians have formed hundreds of associations dedicated to community welfare, cultural identity, ethnic solidarity, or to particular local concerns such as education and infrastructure that are neglected by government. For instance, during our visit, we met with representatives of an association from eastern Nigeria. Members of the association working in Lagos and abroad had sponsored several improvements in their home villages as well as scholarships for promising students. Individually, the constituents of groups like this one are usually oriented to parochial issues; collectively, they represent a large sphere of grassroots activity. These organizations are especially important for articulating community problems, promoting local interests with the government, and interacting with other communities. In a democratic context, they could play important roles in representation and mediation.

In general, few of these civic organizations have taken an assertive political role. At the most inclusive level, Community Action for Popular Participation (CAPP), a nonpartisan group with a diverse membership, has championed the rights and activities of grassroots organizations and agitated for a more open civic arena. Organizations in some localities have provided tacit support for national political movements, influenced largely by the community's particular relation to the military regime, whether toward cooperation with the official political parties or toward support for dissident groups. In general, though, local associations are politically cautious, however varied the activities they sponsor. The more explicitly political organizations have experienced government surveillance and repression, most conspicuously in the Ogoni region.

RECOMMENDATIONS

Members of these organizations also strongly conveyed to the study mission the challenges of isolation, parochialism, and fragmentation. Such problems suggest a useful role in promoting affinities among groups and involving Nigerian organizations more fully in international networks. Many Nigerian organizations have linkages with international counterparts, notably in the areas of the environment, women's rights, health care, grassroots development, and academia. Building upon these existing relationships is an obvious starting point, and extending alliances with labor, students, and various professionals is also important.

Foundations, donor agencies, and international organizations should increase support for efforts by these groups to meet and communicate among themselves, whether on the basis of disparate issues (for example, children's health or the environment) or among a broader community of civic groups. Opportunities to share experiences and develop common strategies will be invaluable for Nigeria's popular organizations. In addition, there must be assertive outreach to support Nigerian participation in international visitors' and exchange programs, fellowships, and training activities. Finally, in view of the uneven relationships between civic associations and government, there may be a need to defend particular groups and individuals. While many organizations have worked without direct constraints, others have been subject to harassment and abuse. It is essential for concerned outsiders to try to halt government persecution and restrictions and to defend the activities of independent associations.

CONFLICT RESOLUTION GROUPS

As political and social stresses have given rise to a growing array of conflicts in Nigeria, a succession of military regimes have shown little inclination or ability to alleviate such tensions. Indeed, they have at times aggravated tension, as they do by creating new states and local governments without prior consultation. More recently, some initiative in the area of conflict resolution has been evident within civil society. A small but active core of nongovernmental organizations is dedicated to work in this area. These groups pursue various activities, including early warning efforts to identify potential local conflicts, research on mechanisms for alleviating conflict domestically and in the West African region, training of counselors and arbitrators for intervention in disputes, and the creation of networks for dialogue among different communities.

By and large, the efforts of conflict resolution groups have not been overtly political, and most have not encountered significant interference from the authorities. However, as a leading member of one organization remarked to our group, "To prevent conflict in Nigeria, we need to strengthen democratic institutions. They allow bargaining and negotiation. We must remove from the psychology of people that they need a military regime to solve problems." He also stressed the need to develop relations between civil society and the government. "In a military regime, they tend to think anyone outside of government is subversive. But we could build bridges to government, not necessarily subvert it." The work of conflict resolution groups naturally becomes more challenging as economic and political uncertainties give rise to increasing levels of conflict throughout Nigerian society. This field of activity has recently appeared to be one of the more vibrant and promising areas in civil society.

RECOMMENDATIONS

There are numerous possibilities for external linkages with Nigerian conflict resolution groups. A number of academics, universities, and programs have connections to Nigeria. These should be developed, possibly with a view toward building a more cohesive transnational web of institutions. International NGOs oriented toward conflict resolution should extend their activities in Nigeria and seek out regular contact with Nigerian institutions. This recommendation applies to grant-making institutions, which can support communications facilities, research capabilities, and Nigerian participation in international activities, as well as to research and practitioner groups that can establish stronger relations with conflict resolution organizations. Official donors and multilateral institutions are important as well, notably in sponsoring conferences and exchanges. In addition, it is important for outsiders to identify notables in Nigeria—whether government leaders, traditional rulers, politicians, local activists, or other civic figures —who can play important roles as mediators and advisers in conflict situations. These individuals should be brought into a networking process. Synergies Africa, for instance, a Geneva-based NGO, sponsored a meeting of traditional leaders from northern Nigeria and several neighboring countries to discuss mediation and conflict resolution. Such initiatives could be expanded.

THE MEDIA

The importance of vigorous independent media to democratic development is well understood and requires little elaboration. The scrutiny of the press is essential to instilling accountability among government officials and bolstering political knowledge and engagement among citizens. A wide arena of debate and information are basic ingredients of public discourse. The autonomous media are quite simply a primary agent of pluralism and the foundation of a viable democracy.

Nigeria can boast one of the oldest, largest, and most professionalized media sectors in Africa. Dozens of independent newspapers and magazines are published in Nigeria, and several large publishing groups have a high profile. The domestic market is sufficient to carry a substantial news industry. In recent years, however, government repression has seriously hindered press freedoms and eroded professional morale in this sector. In addition, as in many other countries, while print media enjoy a certain degree of independence, government dominates the much more pervasive electronic broadcast media, radio and television.

THE PRESS AND THE JOURNALISTIC PROFESSION

The print media have historically been dominated by private outlets, with a substantial degree of independence and political engagement. The electronic media are still predominantly controlled by government. Recent economic liberalization measures have allowed for private television and radio stations, but these are mainly commercial operations with little political role.

The press has operated under considerable duress in recent years. The government has promulgated restrictive decrees governing the media and has backed the formation of a government-sponsored media council to monitor professional activities. In 1993 General Babangida issued a decree proscribing four of the country's leading publications, and General Abacha decreed the closure of three major newspaper groups for several months in 1994 and 1995. Among the publishing industry at large, editions have often been confiscated by police; several editorial offices have been ransacked by security agencies, and at least one organization was targeted by unknown arsonists. Alex Ibru, publisher of the *Guardian* newspaper and a member of Abacha's first cabinet, was severely wounded in an unexplained shooting incident in February 1996. On February 26, 1998, Tunde Oladepo, a journalist, was killed by unidentified gunmen. In addition, numerous publishers, editors, and journalists have been detained without trial or charged with criminal offenses.

Despite these constraints, the print media continue to function with a degree of autonomy and dynamism. New publications have appeared in recent years, some of which assume an independent editorial stance. While working under risky conditions, many editors and journalists continue to cover important and even controversial public issues. The editor of a prominent independent publication commented to us on this tension: "When I talk to my counterparts in other African countries they are shocked about what we can publish [in Nigeria]." Nonetheless, he observed, "This is not removed from the fact that we are operating in an oppressive atmosphere. The military are not tolerant. Patience is in short supply in military circles. If you probe anything they regard as information [for] them alone, they arrest you. We are all used to that. . . . We are not told, don't publish. But they want our sources."

The Nigerian Union of Journalists (NUJ) has sought to protect the rights of journalists and the independence of the profession, mainly by defending individuals and arguing against stringent government controls. By keeping to professional issues, the NUJ has been able to voice its concerns without provoking overt reprisals from the authorities. The leading civil liberties organizations have also taken up issues of press freedom, and the Lagos-based Media Rights Agenda (MRA) has been active in this area.

RECOMMENDATIONS

A clear priority for the international community is to support Nigerians in defending and preserving an independent media sector. Nigerian media professionals are already involved in international professional networks, exchanges, and fellowships. While these activities should obviously continue, the outstanding need in Nigeria lies less in the area of professional development than in the areas of legal and political rights. Organizations such as Amnesty International, Human Rights Watch, the Committee to Protect Journalists, and International PEN have taken up the cases of detained journalists and editors. Governments and multilateral organizations such as UNCTAD and the European Union should address press freedom issues as well. Pilot projects in independent electronic media, such as now exist throughout the former Soviet Union, will be essential whenever the political situation permits them. For now the only such effort is the opposition-backed "Radio Kudirat," named for Chief Abiola's assassinated wife, which broadcasts from outside the country.

THE RELIGIOUS DIMENSION

Religion plays an important and often central role in the lives of most Nigerians. The country's religious domain is diverse. The pattern of religious identities in Nigeria is somewhat clouded by mixed patterns of observance and the lack of clear statistics. It is generally accepted that, nationally, 45–50 percent of the population practices some form of Islam, 40–45 percent are nominally Christian, and the balance follow traditional religions. These are not mutually exclusive categories, as many people combine "mainstream" doctrine with elements of indigenous practice.

There are substantial religious variations across Nigeria. The states of the far north (several of which, in the northwest, are successors of the nineteenth-century emirates established by Usman dan Fodio) are overwhelmingly Muslim. In these areas Islam has been an integral part of the state structure for about two centuries, and political and religious leadership have often been fused. Parts of northern Nigeria were more closely linked to Sudan and the Arab world through trans-Saharan trade routes than to the West African coastal societies. The southeastern zones, including Igbo areas and many minorities, are predominantly Christian. The Yoruba people of the southwest are almost equally divided among Christians and Muslims, and they have exhibited a unique degree of religious accord. In that region Islam has spread through traders and proselytizers rather than through an Islamic state and has never been as closely intertwined with political power. Many Yoruba families include both Christians and Muslims, and intermarriage is common. The states of the middle belt, home to various minorities, are also religiously diverse, but this area has emerged as a spiritual, and sometimes physical, battleground in recent years as competition over conversions has combined with conflicts over land and political power.

Surveying the range of religious activity and the implications for political life, it is important to make two distinctions, the first of which concerns the goals of religious groupings. Most religious communities are devoted primarily to matters of faith, although many have taken up issues of social welfare or considerations of justice and equity. Consequently, there are a range of secular interests joined with spiritual pursuits.

There is also an important distinction between hierarchical and localized religious organizations. Hierarchical groupings include the major "established" denominations and doctrines. They embody a large-scale organization and a set of authority relations among leaders and adherents. Localized groupings focus mainly on the needs of a particular community.

In recent years, there has been evident a growth of religious activity in Nigeria, especially at the local level. The clearest reasons for this are the quest for meaning and community in difficult economic or political circumstances and the attraction of the social services provided by some religious groups. Religious mobilization presents different facets: certain communities eschew worldly concerns, while others either uphold or challenge the existing social and political order. Moreover, some people within the Christian and Muslim communities—mainly among the localized groupings—have actively confronted neighboring religious communities, causing tension and conflict in recent years.

Nigeria's religious landscape includes the following features:

Muslim Organizations

The Islamic community in Nigeria is diverse, encompassing orthodoxy, heterodoxy, and a variety of reform movements. Nigerian Muslims are overwhelmingly identified with the Sunni tradition of the Maliki school, which predominates in West Africa. The hierarchical domain of Islam is defined by a few peak associations, Sufi orders, and emirates. The leading associations include the Nigerian Supreme Council for Islamic Affairs (NSCIA) and the Federation of Muslim Women's Associations of Nigeria (FOMWAN). The peak federations are the most inclusive in ethnic and regional scope. These are modern civic organizations based on religious identity rather than religious organizations per se. In terms of practice, the Qadiriyya and Tijaniyya Sufi orders claim wide adherence in the north, as do the networks of ulama (Islamic scholars) based in the northern emirates. Some of the leaders of orthodox Islam, especially in the north, receive government salaries or subsidy, including both the judges (qadis) of shari'a courts and the traditional rulers of the emirates. This link to the state restricts their capacity for independent political action. State enforcement of shari'a also provides a source of legitimacy independent of democracy for some Muslims.

Some Muslim leaders have collaborated with their Christian counterparts in efforts to resolve religious conflict and reduce communal tensions. A proponent of such efforts from the Muslim community discussed with our group the hazards and possibilities for interaction: "The meeting point [for dialogue] is that Nigeria is a multi-religious country. We recognize religious matters, providing nothing is done to hinder the freedom of worship. No undue advantage should be given to one religion by government. It should be fair, not uniform . . . There is a strong school of opinion that we need a platform for dealing together [Muslims and Christians] more at the local level." He added, however, that "the present government is not really inclined for dialogue."

The localized organizations of Islam have been more controversial in political and social terms, though here again there is considerable diversity. Alongside the existing reformist movement known as the yan'Izala, a number of autonomous mosques have emerged in recent years, many reportedly linked to the growth of the Ikhwan or Muslim Brothers. There are several related though distinct phenomena in the growth of grassroots Muslim movements in northern Nigeria. First, many independent preachers have founded their own mosques, often in poorer sections of the cities. There mosques provide some social services and could serve as a base for political mobilization. At the same time, activists have organized a political movement at universities, madrasas and elsewhere modeled on the Muslim Brotherhood format. One of the movement's founders, Ibrahim Zakzaky, was educated in Iran, leading to the misnomer "Shi'ite" for the movement. "They call them Shi'ites by association," remarked a senior Muslim leader to our group. The study mission was told in Kano that the movement had split. Its links to the independent mosques are unclear. The Ikhwan is the most contentious of the localized entities, reflecting a militant form of religious mobilization. Sustained economic hardship and rising inequalities have fed dislocation and social frustration, fostering the growth of Islamist movements. Like the yan'Tatsine ("Maitatsine") movement, a heterodox sect that staged a bloody uprising in Kano in the early 1980s, the followers of Sheik Zakzaky have increasingly come into direct conflict with northern authorities. The reported reappearance of yan'Tatsine followers in Lagos has also been a matter of official concern. The regime regards these sects with consternation and has acted to repress the more militant groups.

CHRISTIAN ORGANIZATIONS

The leading Christian denominations are the Roman Catholic church and the "mainstream" Protestants, including Anglicans, Methodists, Presbyterians, and Baptists. These groups are all represented in the umbrella Christian Association of Nigeria (CAN), along with the more localized and heterodox Aladuras (a syncretic church including elements of Yoruba religion) and—until their recent separation as an independent grouping—the Pentecostals. The mainstream Protestant denominations are also grouped in the Christian Conference of Nigeria (CCN). The largest hierarchical Christian groupings, heavily concentrated in the southern states, have been assertive in voicing concerns over political democracy, social justice, and human rights.

Both Catholic and Anglican hierarchies have issued appeals for peace, political dialogue, and increased liberties. In a recent example, following the arrests of mainly Yoruba military officers in December 1997, the Anglican bishop called for a week of fasting to save the country from crisis.[2] Major denominations, including Catholics, Anglicans, Pentecostals, and Presbyterians, refused to join a national prayer on behalf of the regime's transition program in May 1998.[3] In addition, several Christian leaders have sought cooperation with Muslim notables in conflict resolution and interfaith accord. One principal in these efforts, from a major denomination, emphasized to participants in the study mission, "It is not so much a matter of dialogue or theological discussion. It should be standard that Muslims and Christians meet together normally, and not wait until there is a crisis . . . One thing we have in common is that we both want to take our faith seriously. We are concerned about the way the country is going with corruption and bad influences."

Localized Christian groupings include the Aladura, Cherubim and Seraphim, the Pentecostals, and numerous independent churches. Just as independent mosques have proliferated among Muslims, so have independent churches among Christians. One Nigerian characterized these churches as a "business" for enterprising unemployed, educated youth, but some at least appear to meet genuine social and spiritual needs. The Pentecostals have experienced substantial growth along with other evangelical or charismatic churches. Foreign evangelical groups have made significant headway, especially beyond the traditional, southern Christian zones. Most of these have been oriented toward personal salvation and proselytizing rather than social issues. Some of the local groups have come into conflict with Muslim communities, particularly in the middle belt. A few Catholic clergy have been attracted to the Latin American model of religious base communities and social mobilization, though most such efforts are relatively new.

THE ROLE OF RELIGION

Religious groupings have a special importance in Nigerian politics and society. At the mass level, these affiliations are often important in defining communal relations. Among Nigerian elites, religious leaders enjoy considerable latitude in speaking to social and political issues. This suggests that religious communities can play constructive roles in promoting change, resolving conflict, and advancing reform.[4] At the same time, there is considerable potential for dissension or division, as witnessed in national controversies over religion and clashes among different communities, such as the disputes in the late 1970s over the application of shari'a and in the mid-1980s over Nigeria's membership in the Organization of the Islamic Conference (OIC). In the past few years hundreds of people have died in local conflicts among Muslims and Christians in several northern and middle-belt towns: Kaduna, Katsina, Bauchi, Kafanchan, Zangon-Kataf, and Tafawa Balewa. These disputes usually begin over land, commercial rivalries, or local disputes and escalate into religious clashes. As a northern academic observed, "[There is a] reassertion of identities we thought were no longer significant. People are reasserting ethnic, religious, and communal identities. They are becoming a platform for mobilization rather than the Nigerian identity."

Religious communities maintain contacts with the state, with other national or local religious groups, and with international associations. The hierarchical religious establishments have carried on dialogue with the government. As noted above, several Christian denominations such as the Anglicans, Catholics, and Methodists have urged greater respect for human rights, genuine democratization, and political reconciliation between government and opposition. These groups have also sought improvements in equity and social welfare. The military regime has reacted with indifference to most of these overtures. Religious leaders could nonetheless play a role, under the appropriate circumstances, as intermediaries for reconciliation or accord between government and opposition.

There have been periodic attempts at interfaith dialogue and interreligious cooperation. In the wake of the OIC controversy, in 1987 the government sponsored an Advisory Council on Religious Affairs to promote accord between Christians and Muslims, but it quickly fell dormant. In an account offered by a Muslim participant, "We recommended a joint [Christian and Muslim] Chair. But there was a military regime, so we had to have one leader, and we agreed on a rotation. But that formula eventually made the organization sink into inaction." Direct contacts have been opened between peak associations such as the Christian Association of Nigeria and the Nigerian Supreme Council for Islamic Affairs, accompanied by less formal discussions among senior clerics. The recent, quiet dialogue between a high-ranking, Abuja-based Christian clergyman and his northern Muslim counterpart provides an example that has been duplicated in other instances. Some prominent Muslims have been amenable to these initiatives. "I don't think Muslims are averse to that kind of relationship," commented a senior Islamic leader in our discussions. "I believe it should be given proper attention, at both national and state levels . . . The Advisory Council on Religious Affairs should be revived; it should not be advisory but decision-making." These overtures have had constructive purposes in trying to regularize exchanges and increase understanding among principal religious authorities. But such efforts have been ad hoc and sporadic, and they have not developed a stable network of communication among clergy and religious leaders.

At the grassroots level, members of different religious traditions—clerics, educators, activists, and community leaders—have encouraged communication and tried to alleviate communal conflict. Conflict resolution groups have trained counselors and mediators of different faiths to intercede in local disputes. These groups, although small, show considerable promise in helping to mitigate the eruption of strife or halt its spread.

Apart from issues of interfaith relations and conflict resolution, religious groups also serve important coping functions in difficult economic conditions. Charitable activities and social welfare are an important source of sustenance for many marginalized communities. A senior clergyman in a leading Christian denomination described this obligation in detail to the study group:

> The church sees poverty and the deteriorating social situation first hand. At [my residence], there is no day we do not have six or seven people asking for assistance. They have no money for food, for hospital bills. We do the little we can, but this is not a solution . . . the church can do very little. They try to bring this to the attention of the government.

From an international perspective, the religious sphere in Nigeria is substantially different from most other areas of nongovernmental organization. Along with their large membership and extensive organization, Christians and Muslims have strong networks among foreign religious establishments and some ecumenical and interfaith associations. They can draw upon financial and organizational resources not available to most civic groups. Christian communities in Nigeria have firm ties to various international churches, a number of African-American denominations among them, and to other individual congregations or parishes, sometimes through the presence of Nigerian Christians resident abroad.[5] In addition, many groups are active in ecumenical associations such as the World Council of Churches. Nigerian Muslims also maintain extensive relations with West Africa and the wider Islamic world, especially Saudi Arabia. Contacts with the Muslim community in the United States, Europe, and southern Africa have been less extensive or regular.

RECOMMENDATIONS

There are few signs of systematic religious discrimination in Nigeria, but dissident voices of any faith are often suppressed. While recognizing that a legally constituted government has a right to counter violent or illegal acts, it is essential for those concerned with the practice of religion in Nigeria to support the same rights and freedoms for all branches of civil society. Many external parties—governments, multilateral organizations, human rights groups, and religious entities—have a role to play in defending these prerogatives.

Most important, however, is for international religious organizations to work with Nigeria partners in their efforts to become agents of change rather than forces for division. As in other authoritarian states, religious organizations are now virtually the only institutions with grassroots networks, public legitimacy, and independence. Religious communities and ideals can provide a powerful force for change. In multiconfessional Nigeria, however, religious mobilization is more problematic than in more uniform societies such as Poland or Haiti. Without interreligious dialogue it can lead to division rather than cooperation, as it ultimately did, for instance, in British India. But if religious leaders and communities can cooperate across confessional and sectarian lines, they can make a significant difference. International religious communities have a special role to play in supporting efforts at dialogue and interfaith action in Nigeria. One way is through direct partnership with Nigerian clergy and organizations. It is also important to provide opportunities for broader interaction between Christian and Muslim communities through meetings in Nigeria or outside the country. These endeavors could focus on areas of confidence building among different denominations and regional groups, as well as seeking vehicles for conflict resolution in the religious sphere.

THE BUSINESS COMMUNITY

As one business leader remarked to our study group, "There is no reason for Nigeria to be a 'developing' country." A distinguished journalist observed that Nigeria is a "rich country full of poor people." Both were expressing their frustration at the nation's unfulfilled economic potential. The government has garnered more than $280 billion in oil revenues over the past twenty-five years. The country has a large internal market and has trained a growing pool of skilled people. Yet per capita income has dropped by nearly three-quarters since the early 1980s, and Nigeria has slipped from middle-income status back to the ranks of the low-income developing countries. While adverse global markets have affected Nigeria's fortunes, economic stagnation results mainly from prolonged mismanagement and political instability.

Nigeria's overly centralized economy is a primary source of political dissension, while economic malaise has aggravated social frustration and conflict. Economic reform is an important foundation for political stability. A vigorous private sector can revitalize Nigeria's economy while providing the basis for more equitable and decentralized growth. The business community possesses resources and expertise, yet much-needed investments will not be forthcoming without a better commercial environment. The private sector, both domestic and foreign, has a crucial role to play in demanding improved economic governance.

The organized private sector is among the more vital and less constrained components of civic organization in Nigeria. The resources of the business community, its links to members of government, and its ability to focus narrowly on issues of economic performance have all served to maintain a dialogue between peak business associations and the regime. Some private sector groups have been concerned with issues of corruption and political liberalization as important adjuncts to economic reform, while others have preserved a "technical" focus on matters of economic policy and institutional change.

Memberships and networks overlap considerably among the business community, but it is possible to distinguish between the traditional business interest associations and a newer set of organizations. The older groups, some with roots going back to the early colonial period, include the Lagos Chamber of Commerce and Industry (LCCI), the Nigerian Association of Chambers of Commerce, Industry, Mines, and Agriculture (NACCIMA), and the Manufacturers' Association of Nigeria (MAN). The latter two are peak associations, while the LCCI is one of several dozen local chambers of commerce, most of which participate under the NACCIMA umbrella. The chambers in various locations differ in the amount of resources they command and the stances they take, with the LCCI and a few other local groups among the most active. NACCIMA leaders have vocally advocated political liberalization as requisite for economic progress in Nigeria, although the association has primarily concerned itself with the economic policy environment. The MAN has not stood out as much, owing to weaker organization and less effective policy recommendations.

Within the past few years, a new set of business interest groups has appeared. Many of these have strong ties to the international business community and dynamic local entrepreneurs. The Enabling Environment Forum (EEF) and the West Africa Enterprise Network (WAEN) are important examples of groups that have pressed for a more open economic setting and greater engagement between Nigeria and the world economy. The Center for Public-Private Cooperation (CPPC) is another organization working to improve dialogue over economic strategy.

The leading organization of this type is the Nigerian Economic Summit, which brings together major domestic and foreign private sector interests in dialogue with senior government officials over broad issues of economic change. It aspires to a think tank model rather than that of a competitive new business association, and since 1993 it has sponsored a series of high-visibility meetings and publications covering all sectors and activities in the economy. The summit is apparently moving toward an institutionalized process of public-private sector consultation, with important implications for the entire organized private sector. The Vision 2010 forum is a direct outcome of the summit agenda and a further development of the consultative process between business and government. While the summits and Vision 2010 have stayed clear of overt political recommendations, concerns over improved governance have been raised by participants in several meetings. The important part government plays in both removes them from the realm of civil society as it is understood in pluralistic political systems. They more resemble the official, government-sponsored consultation in corporatist systems.

The foreign business community includes a large number of firms and activities, although external investment is overwhelmingly concentrated in the oil sector. International firms are members of NAC-CIMA and MAN, among others, and a few companies have been active in the economic summits and Vision 2010 forums. During the recent crises, foreign businesses have maintained their traditional distance from overt political engagement, generally keeping a low profile and trying to sustain their commercial activities. Several of the major oil companies, notably Royal Dutch/Shell, have been embroiled in disputes with local communities in the producing areas and have attracted criticism worldwide for their conduct with regard to the Ogoni. Inspired by the movement for sanctions against apartheid South Africa, an international initiative has been started to boycott and impose sanctions on companies that do business in Nigeria under the military regime. Partly in response to these and other pressures, Shell has publicly released a new business code addressing such issues as human rights and environmental concerns. It has also announced an intention to direct greater resources to local community development in its producing areas. Other companies, such as Chevron and Mobil, have dealt with sporadic local violence or environmental problems on an ad hoc basis, often relying upon the government to resolve such issues.

RECOMMENDATIONS

Foreign corporations are principally concerned with preserving stable commercial relationships, and they generally refrain from public involvement in political issues in their host countries. In their home countries, however, they are often more vocal. Mobil, for instance, has strongly opposed the imposition of economic sanctions as a tool of foreign policy. At the same time, the business community is affected by corruption and policy uncertainty and has an interest in improving economic governance. It is possible, and even necessary, for international companies to engage with Nigerian civil society in order to improve the commercial environment over the longer term. The most direct avenue of involvement is active participation in the economic summit process and other forums such as Vision 2010. These outlets offer investors opportunities to advocate improvements in administration and policy. Close partnership with Nigerian business associations also can support the cause of the domestic private sector on issues of common concern. As noted previously, however, such forums have limited value in a context of authoritarian, unaccountable governancy.

In addition, foreign investors can help to strengthen the nongovernmental sector by assisting grassroots development efforts through local associations. Corporations can help to establish and finance community foundations, which channel funds through certified NGOs in particular areas. This can be an effective, politically neutral method for supporting community welfare and improving relations with different localities while also building a sustainable capacity for grassroots activity.

International donors can have an important influence on the course of change. Resources can be directed to nongovernmental organizations working for general improvements in entrepreneurship and the business climate. Over the longer term, in the event of political change, it may be possible for bilateral and multilateral donors to offer inducements such as debt relief, concessional lending, and supplementary finance for major new investments in support of economic recovery under a democratic government.

While there is an understandable reluctance by foreign companies to express political views, those with a major stake in Nigeria's development should take an interest in more stable and legitimate governance. One way to advance these aims is to support the efforts of Nigerian colleagues, whether in the business associations or as members of NGOs such as Transparency International, which works against corruption. Another outlet is to pursue quiet dialogue with government officials over issues of civil liberties, minority rights, and a stable transition to civilian rule. Major foreign investors can use their unique access to senior officials to counsel the importance of credible and prompt reform.

Since 1993, a leading concern of foreign firms active in Nigeria has been to avoid the imposition of sanctions on trade and investment with that country. The oil industry has led such efforts. It is natural that petroleum companies would oppose an oil embargo. Nonetheless, it is important to recognize the considerable medium- to long-term political risks faced by international firms under the status quo. These risks are of several sorts: the possibility of greater instability, with increasingly adverse effects on operations; a consequent introduction of more stringent sanctions by foreign countries; and opposition in the consuming countries stemming from a growing sanctions movement. Therefore, we believe it is in the best interests of firms doing business in Nigeria to be forward-looking and to take steps to encourage more stable and legitimate governance. Collaboration with civil society in the areas described here can be a significant step in this process, but it is equally important that the international oil firms at least not obstruct efforts by governments to pressure the military regime, even if some of the policy instruments used conflict with the companies' immediate economic interests. If they do so, they can expect more outspoken opposition from activist groups, including boycotts.

CONCLUSION

When we started this project, many people warned us it would be difficult. Few, however, predicted how rewarding it would be and even how encouraging, despite the immense obstacles to change in Nigeria.

The level of corruption and institutional decay in Nigeria is matched by a unique energy in the NGO sector and civil society generally. Oil wealth empowers authoritarian and exclusionary governments and inhibits some forms of international action against them, but it also assures the country of a degree of high-level diplomatic attention. The nation's size and complexity present many opportunities for conflict but have also bred a hard-won appreciation of diversity and federalism. With a growing impetus from the grassroots (assisted by its international connections), Nigeria can still change course. As the Roman Catholic archbishop of Jos said in his invocation at the opening of Vision 2010: "We thank God for a country rich in human and material resources. And we confess that we have wasted both. But God permits U-turns."

APPENDIXES

— Appendix A —

ABOUT THE AUTHORS

PETER M. LEWIS is an assistant professor at American University's School of International Service and has also taught at Michigan State University. His research and writings focus on economic reform and political transition in Nigeria and sub-Saharan Africa. He directed the Center for Preventive Action's project on Nigeria.

PEARL T. ROBINSON is the director of the Program on International Relations and an associate professor of political science at Tufts University. She is also an adjunct associate professor at the Fletcher School of Law and Diplomacy. She has written extensively on democratization, reform, and transition politics in Africa.

BARNETT R. RUBIN is a senior fellow and the director of the Center for Preventive Action at the Council on Foreign Relations. He was an associate professor of political science and director of the Center for the Study of Central Asia at Columbia University from 1990 to 1996. Previously, he was a fellow at the United States Institute of Peace and taught at Yale University. His research has primarily been concerned with conflict prevention, state formation, and human rights in Asia and Africa.

— Appendix B —

NIGERIA WORKING GROUP

C. NANA-OYE ADDO-YOBO*
Legon Centre for International Affairs,
University of Ghana

JAMES E. BAKER
Long Island University

HARRY BARNES, JR.
Carter Center

SALIH BOOKER
Council on Foreign Relations

DAVID CORTRIGHT
Fourth Freedom Forum

M. WILLIAM HOWARD, JR.
New York Theological Seminary

PETER M. LEWIS*
American University

GEORGE A. LOPEZ
University of Notre Dame

PAUL E. LOVEJOY
York University

* Participated in the study mission to Nigeria in January 1997.

VIVIAN LOWERY DERRYCK
Africa Leadership Forum/Academy for Educational Development

DARREN KEW*
Fletcher School of Law and Diplomacy

GWENDOLYN MIKELL
Georgetown University

JOHN N. PADEN*
George Mason University

DAVID L. PHILLIPS
International Conflict Resolution Program,
Columbia University

PEARL T. ROBINSON*
Tufts University

BARNETT R. RUBIN*
Center for Preventive Action,
Council on Foreign Relations

DONALD W. SHRIVER, JR.
Union Theological Seminary

JOHN J. STREMLAU
Carnegie Commission on Preventing Deadly Conflict

JOHN L. WASHBURN
Washington Working Group on the International Criminal Court

L. KIRK WOLCOTT
Carter Center

* Participated in the study mission to Nigeria in January 1997.

— Appendix C —

CIVIL SOCIETY
ORGANIZATIONS IN NIGERIA

T he following is a selected list of civil society organizations in
Nigeria. It includes organizations mentioned in the text, as well as
others that have been active and prominent in recent years. Because of
the fluid situation in Nigeria and the effects of government repression,
not all of these groups may still be active. The list is not comprehensive
in most sectors, especially in the areas of religion, labor, and local or ethnic associations. Some groups are listed in more than one category.

DEMOCRACY, HUMAN RIGHTS, AND LAW

HUMAN RIGHTS AND DEMOCRACY ORGANIZATIONS

African Democratic Heritage (ADHERE)
African Democratic League (ADL)
African Redemption Movement (ARM)
Amnesty International Nigeria
Association for Democracy and Good Governance in Nigeria (ADGN)
Campaign for Democracy (CD)
Civil Liberties Organization (CLO)
Committee for the Defense of Human Rights (CDHR)
Community Action for Popular Participation (CAPP)
Concerned Professionals (CP)
Constitutional Rights Project (CRP)

Council for Public Education (CPE)
Democratic Action Committee (DACOM)
Democratic Alternative (DA)
Democratic Forum (DF)
Freedom Charter International (FCI)
Gani Fawehinmi Solidarity Organization (GFSA)
Human Rights Africa (HRA)
Human Rights Committee (HRC)
Institute of Human Rights and Humanitarian Law (IHR/HL)
Joint Action Committee of Nigeria (JACON)
Kaduna Alliance for Democracy (KAD)
Labor and Youth Defense Committee (LYDC)
Mahmud Tukur Memorial Committee (MTMC)
Movement for Democracy and Development in Africa (MDDA)
Movement for National Reformation (MNR)
Movement for Popular Democracy (MPD)
Movement for Social and Economic Justice (MOSEJ)
Movement for the Survival of the Ogoni People (MOSOP)
Movement for Unity and Progress (MUP)
National Association for Democratic Citizens (NADC)
National Committee of Patriots (NCOP)
National Conscience Party (NCP)
National Democratic Coalition (NADECO)
National Solidarity Group in Defense of Democracy (NSGDD)
Nigeria Collective Council (NCC)
Nigerianity Movement (NM)
People's Committee for Liberty (PCL)
The Progressive Movement for Democracy (PMD)
Uhuru Research Center (URC)
United Action for Democracy (UAD)
United Democratic Front of Nigeria (UDFN)
Unity Forum for Peace and Democracy (UFPD)
Universal Defenders of Democracy (UDD)
Young Democrats (YD)

THE LEGAL PROFESSION

International Association of Female Lawyers (FIDA)
National Association of Democratic Lawyers (NADL)
Nigeria Bar Association (NBA)

UMBRELLA GROUPS

African Network for Democracy (AFRONET)
Campaign for Democracy (CD)
Democratic Alternative (DA)
National Consultative Forum (NCF)
The 100 Group Nigeria
United Action for Democracy (UAD)

EXTERNAL GROUPS

Center for Democratic Development (CDD)
Coalition of Democratic Awareness (CDA)
Joint Action Committee (JACOM)
Justice Nigeria
MOSOP-UK
NADECO-Abroad
National Alliance for Democracy (NAD)
National Democratic Alliance Committee (NDAC)
National Freedom Front (NFF)
National Liberation Council of Nigeria (NALICON)
New Nigeria Forum (NNF)
Nigeria Democratic Movement (NDM)
Nigerian Liberation Group (NLG)
Nigerian Welfare and Monitoring Council
United Democratic Front of Nigeria

POPULAR ASSOCIATIONS

LABOR ORGANIZATIONS (SELECTED)

Campaign for Independent Unionism (CIU)
Campaign for Workers' Alternative (CWA)
Iron and Steel Senior Staff Association (ISSSA)
Medical and Health Workers Union of Nigeria (MHWUN)
National Union of Air Transport Service Employees (NUATSE)
National Union of Petroleum and Natural Gas Workers (NUPENG)
National Union of Public Corporation Employees (NUPCE)

Nigerian Labour Congress (NLC)
Petroleum and Natural Gas Senior Staff Association of Nigeria (PEN-
GASSAN)

WOMEN'S ORGANIZATIONS

Empowerment and Action Research Centre (EMPARC)
Federation of Muslim Women's Associations of Nigeria (FOMWAN)
National Council of Women's Societies (NCWS)
Women Concerned (WC)
Women in Nigeria (WIN)

STUDENTS AND ACADEMICS

Academic Staff Union of Universities (ASUU)
National Association of Nigerian Students (NANS)
Nigeria Philosophy Association (NPA)
Non-Academic Staff Union of Universities (NASU)
Senior Staff Association of Nigerian Universities (SSANU)

ENVIRONMENTAL GROUPS

Environmental Rights Action-CLO
Maroko Evacuees Committee (MEC)
Movement for the Survival of the Ogoni People (MOSOP)

THE MEDICAL PROFESSION

Medical and Health Workers Union of Nigeria (MHWUN)
National Association of Nigerian Nurses and Midwives (NANNM)
Nigerian Medical Association (NMA)

THE MEDIA

Association of Nigerian Authors (ANA)
Media Rights Agenda (MRA)
Newspaper Distributors Association of Nigeria (NDAN)
Nigerian Union of Journalists (NUJ)
The Independent Print Media

LOCAL AND ETHNIC ASSOCIATIONS

Ethnic Minority Rights Organization of Africa (EMIROAF)
Mainland Progressive Youth Movement (MPYM)
Maroko Evacuees Committee (MEC)
Movement for the Survival of the Ogoni People (MOSOP)
National Youth Council of the Ogoni People (NYCOP)
Nigerian Tenants Association (NTA)

RELIGIOUS ORGANIZATIONS
(umbrella/peak associations)

MUSLIM

Nigerian Supreme Council for Islamic Affairs (NSCIA)
Federation of Muslim Women's Associations of Nigeria (FOMWAN)

CHRISTIAN

Christian Association of Nigeria (CAN)
Christian Conference of Nigeria (CCN)

BUSINESS ASSOCIATIONS

Center for Public-Private Cooperation (CPPC)
Enabling Environment Forum (EEF)
Lagos Chamber of Commerce and Industry (LCCI); and other local
    chambers of commerce
Manufacturers' Association of Nigeria (MAN)
Nigerian Association of Chambers of Commerce, Industry, Mines, and
    Agriculture (NACCIMA)
Nigerian Economic Summit (NES)
West Africa Enterprise Network (WAEN)

Source: Raufu Mustapha, "Civil Rights and Pro-Democracy Groups in and outside Nigeria," paper presented at a conference on The Nigerian Democratization Process and the European Union, Talence, France, September 12–14, 1996; and authors' compilation.

— Appendix D —

INTERNET RESOURCES ON NIGERIA

There are a large number of Internet sites with information on Nigeria. Some sites with extensive links to information on Nigeria and related resources are listed below.

U.S. Department of State, Human Rights Practices, 1997
www.state.gov/www/global/human_rights/1997_hrp_report/nigeria.html

U.S Department of State, Bureau of African Affairs
www.state.gov/www/regions/africa/index.html

United States Institute of Peace, Special Report on Nigeria
www.usip.org/oc/sr/NigeriaReport.html

National Endowment for Democracy
www.ned.org/

Africa Policy Information Center & Washington Office on Africa
www.africapolicy.org

University of Pennsylvania African Studies, Nigeria Page
www.sas.upenn.edu/African_Studies/Country_Specific/Nigeria.html

Federal Republic of Nigeria
http://tribeca.ios.com/~n123/nigerldr.htm#admin

The Africa News Service
Africa News Online—Nigeria
http://www.africanews.org/west/nigeria/

Association of Concerned Africa Scholars
www.prairienet.org/acas/siro.html

Centre for Democracy and Development
www.cdd.org.uk

The Africa Fund
www.prairienet.org/acas/afund.html

━ Appendix E ━

TRANSITION TIMETABLE ANNOUNCED BY GENERAL ABACHA ON OCTOBER 1, 1995
(WITH PROGRESS ON SOME MEASURES AS OF JUNE 1998)

1995 Fourth Quarter, October–December

Approval of draft constitution (not yet done)

Lifting of all restrictions on political activities (party registration law contradicts this)

Establishment of the National Electoral Commission of Nigeria (NECON)

Appointment of panel for creation of state and local government boundary adjustment

Creation of:

    Transitional Implementation Committee

    National Reconciliation Committee Federal Character Commission

1996 First Quarter January–March

Election and inauguration of local government councils on nonparty basis (convened March 1996)

1996 Second Quarter April–June

Creation of states and local governments (done October 1996)

Commencement of process of political party registration

1996 Third Quarter July–September

Registration of political parties (done; final results announced October 1, 1996)

Delineation of constituencies

Production of authentic voter register

1996 Fourth Quarter October–December
Election of local government councils at party level (conducted March 1997)

1997 First Quarter January–March
Inauguration of party-elected local government councils
Consolidation of new political party structures
Tribunal sitting and conduct of any local government by-elections

1997 Second Quarter April–June
Primary elections select candidates for state assembly and governorship elections
Screening and approval of candidates by the National Electoral Commission

1997 Third Quarter July–September
State assembly elections (conducted December 1997)

1997 Fourth Quarter October–December
Election of state governors (postponed until August 1998)
Sitting of state election tribunals and conduct of by-elections

1998 First Quarter January–March
Inauguration of state assemblies and state governors (postponed)
Party primaries to select candidates for National Assembly elections
National Assembly election campaigns

1998 Second Quarter April–June
National Assembly elections (conducted April 1998)
Commencement of nationwide campaigns for the presidential election

1998 Third Quarter July–Spetember
Presidential election (scheduled to coincide with gubernatorial elections, August 1, 1998)

October 1, 1998
Swearing in of new elected president and final disengagement by military

— Appendix F —

THE ADVISORY BOARD OF THE CENTER FOR PREVENTIVE ACTION

Chair:
JOHN W. VESSEY
former chairman of the Joint
Chiefs of Staff

Vice-Chairs:
FRANCES FITZGERALD
The New Yorker

SAMUEL W. LEWIS
Washington Institute for Near
East Policy

Members:
MORTON I. ABRAMOWITZ
Council on Foreign Relations

GRAHAM T. ALLISON
Harvard University

CRAIG B. ANDERSON
St. Paul's School

JAMES E. BAKER
Long Island University

DENIS A. BOVIN
Bear, Stearns & Company

ANTONIA HANDLER CHAYES
Conflict Management Group

VIVIAN LOWERY DERRYCK
Africa Leadership
Forum/Academy for Educational
Development

ROBERT P. DEVECCHI
Council on Foreign Relations

LESLIE H. GELB (ex officio)
Council on Foreign Relations

LOUIS GERBER
Communications Workers of
America, AFL-CIO

ANDREW J. GOODPASTER
The Eisenhower Institute

ERNEST G. GREEN
Lehman Brothers

RICHARD N. HAASS
The Brookings Institution

SIDNEY HARMAN
Harman International Industries

JAMES W. HARPEL
Harpel Partners, L.P.

ARTHUR HERTZBERG
New York University

JANE E. HOLL
Carnegie Commission on
Preventing Deadly Conflict

SCOTT HORTON
Patterson, Belknap, Webb & Tyler

M. WILLIAM HOWARD, JR.
New York Theological Seminary

HENRY KAUFMAN
Henry Kaufman & Company

RICHARD C. LEONE
The Century Foundation/
Twentieth Century Fund

WENDY W. LUERS
Foundation for a Civil Society

MICHAEL S. LUND
Creative Associates International

ERNEST R. MAY
Harvard University

JAY MAZUR
Union of Needletrades,
Industrial and Textile Employees
(UNITE)

GAY J. MCDOUGALL
International Human Rights Law
Group

DONALD F. MCHENRY
Georgetown University

JOSEPH A. O'HARE, S.J.
Fordham University

PEARL T. ROBINSON
Tufts University

LIONEL A. ROSENBLATT
Refugees International

KENNETH ROTH
Human Rights Watch

KURT L. SCHMOKE
Mayor, City of Baltimore

DONALD W. SHRIVER, JR.
Union Theological Seminary

HEDRICK L. SMITH
Hedrick Smith Productions

JOHN D. STEINBRUNER
The Brookings Institution

FRITZ STERN
Columbia University

JULIA V. TAFT
U.S. Department of State

SEYMOUR TOPPING
Columbia University

HARRY D. TRAIN II
Science Applications
International Corporation

BERNARD E. TRAINOR
Harvard University

ROBERT C. WAGGONER
Burelle's Information Services

MICHAELA WALSH
Women's Asset Management

H. ROY WILLIAMS
U.S. Agency for International
Development

R. JAMES WOOLSEY
Shea & Gardner

ARISTIDE R. ZOLBERG
New School for Social Research

Veronique Albert
Susanna Campbell

NOTES

— 1 —

1. The mission was composed of Pearl T. Robinson of Tufts University, chair of CPA's working group on Nigeria; Barnett R. Rubin, director of CPA; Peter M. Lewis of American University, CPA project director for Nigeria; John N. Paden of George Mason University; and C. Nana-Oye Addo-Yobo, CPA research associate. They were assisted by Darren Kew, then a Fulbright scholar in Nigeria, formerly a CPA research associate.

2. Partial results released by the electoral commission before such releases were stopped by the military government showed a clear trend in Abiola's favor in most regions of the country.

3. The death of General Abacha's son in a plane crash in Kano was also suspected of being an act of terrorism. The balance of the evidence now supports the hypothesis that it was an accident due to pilot error. The suspicions themselves, however, are indicative of the atmosphere.

4. See Segun Adeyemi, "Gambari Says Africa Must Remain Focus of Nigeria's Foreign Policy," Pan African News Agency (New York), April 15, 1997.

5. An insider's account, including many details to which this report cannot do justice, is found in the interview with Omo Omoruyi, published as "The Secret Pact" in *Tell Magazine* (Lagos), September 29, 1997, pp. 14–22, electronic version received from the Nigerian Democratic Movement care of Bolaji Aluko, whose assistance is gratefully acknowledged.

6. For a more detailed analysis, see Human Rights Watch/Africa, "Nigeria: Transition or Travesty? Nigeria's Endless Process of Return to Civilian Rule," *Human Rights Watch* 9, no. 6, (October 1997).

— 3 —

1. This section draws substantially on James S. Coleman, *Nigeria: Background to Nationalism* (Berkeley, Calif.: University of California Press, 1958).

2. Richard Sklar provides an extensive analysis of party dynamics during this period in *Nigerian Political Parties* (Princeton, N.J.: Princeton University Press, 1963).

3. Much of this account is drawn from Larry Diamond, "Nigeria: The Uncivic Society and the Descent into Praetorianism," in Larry Diamond, Juan J. Linz, and Seymour Martin Lipset, eds., *Politics in Developing Countries: Comparing Experiences with Democracy*, 2d ed. (Boulder, Colo.: Lynne Rienner Publishers, 1995). A detailed history of politics in the First Republic is found in Larry Diamond, *Class, Ethnicity, and Democracy in Nigeria: The Failure of the First Republic* (Syracuse: Syracuse University Press, 1988).

4. This period is detailed by Robin Luckham, *The Nigerian Military: A Sociological Analysis of Authority and Revolt 1960–67* (Cambridge: Cambridge University Press, 1971).

5. The title is borrowed from Keith Panter-Brick, ed., *Soldiers and Oil: The Transformation of Nigeria* (London: Frank Cass, 1978). This period is well covered by Anthony Kirk-Greene and Douglas Rimmer, *Nigeria Since 1970: A Political and Economic Outline* (London: Hodder and Stoughton, 1981).

6. These factors are analyzed by Tom Forrest, *Politics and Economic Development in Nigeria*, 2d ed. (Boulder, Colo.: Westview Press, 1995), pp. 133–36.

7. Sayre Schatz, "Pirate Capitalism and the Inert Economy of Nigeria," *Journal of Modern African Studies* 22, no. 1 (March 1984): 45–57.

8. Gavin Williams and Terisa Turner, "Nigeria," in John Dunn, ed., *West African States: Failure and Promise* (Cambridge: Cambridge University Press, 1978).

9. Billy Dudley, *An Introduction to Nigerian Government and Politics* (Bloomington, Ind.: Indiana University Press, 1982), p. 162. This constitutional injunction became a guiding principle not only for electoral competition but also for appointments, employment, and allocations in the public sector.

10. Richard A. Joseph, *Democracy and Prebendal Politics in Nigeria: The Rise and Fall of the Second Republic* (Cambridge: Cambridge University Press, 1987), p. 44.

11. Toyin Falola and Julius Ihonvbere, *The Rise and Fall of Nigeria's Second Republic, 1979–84* (London: Zed Books, 1985), p. 70.

12. Larry Diamond discusses this syndrome as a corrosive feature of politics in the Second Republic; see Larry Diamond, "Cleavage, Conflict and Anxiety in the Second Nigerian Republic," *Journal of Modern African Studies* 20, no. 4 (December 1982): 662.

13. This dynamic is vividly portrayed by Joseph, *Democracy and Prebendal Politics in Nigeria*, passim.

14. Forrest, *Politics and Economic Development in Nigeria*, pp. 83–84.

15. See Diamond, "Nigeria: The Uncivic Society," pp. 468–71.

16. The Buhari-Idiagbon regime is discussed in Forrest, *Politics and Economic Development in Nigeria*, pp. 93–102.

17. Thomas M. Callaghy discusses the genesis of the adjustment program in "Lost between State and Market: The Politics of Economic Adjustment in Ghana, Zambia and Nigeria," in Joan M. Nelson, ed., *Economic Crisis and*

Policy Choice: The Politics of Adjustment in the Third World (Princeton, N.J.: Princeton University Press, 1990), pp. 257–319.

18. The early stages of the transition program have been detailed by Larry Diamond in "Nigeria's Search for a New Political Order," *Journal of Democracy* 2, no. 2 (Spring 1991): 54–69.

19. This section and the next draw heavily on Peter M. Lewis, "Endgame in Nigeria? The Politics of a Failed Democratic Transition," *African Affairs* 93 (July 1994): 323–40.

20. These struggles were detailed in a report by Africa Watch, "Nigeria Contradicting Itself: An Undemocratic Transition Seeks to Bring Democracy Nearer," *Africa Watch*, April 21, 1992, pp. 3–4.

21. The election tabulation was published in most major newspapers and periodicals. See *Newswatch* (Lagos), June 28, 1993, p. 10.

22. Events during the initial years of the Abacha regime are recounted in Diamond, "Nigeria: The Uncivic Society," pp. 460–64, and by Forrest, *Politics and Economic Development in Nigeria*, pp. 240–41.

23. Peter Lewis, "From Prebendalism to Predation: The Political Economy of Decline in Nigeria," *Journal of Modern African Studies* 34, no. 1 (March 1996): 79–103.

24. In fact, there is considerable evidence that senior military officers and their civilian cronies, with heavy involvement in oil transport, garnered a windfall from the crisis. See "Military Machismo," *Africa Confidential* 35, no. 18 (September 1994): 1.

25. Paul Adams, "Reign of the Generals," *Africa Report*, November-December 1994, pp. 27–29.

26. Howard French, "In Nigeria, a Strongman Tightens the Vise," *New York Times*, March 31, 1995, p. A3.

27. The sentence for Yar'Adua was changed to life imprisonment, while Obasanjo received fifteen years.

28. These events are covered in the report by the Civil Liberties Organization, *Annual Report on Human Rights in Nigeria, 1995* (Lagos: Civil Liberties Organization, 1996).

— **4** —

1. This notion has been taken as the title of a report by Human Rights Watch/Africa; see *Permanent Transition: Current Violations of Human Rights in Nigeria* (Washington, D.C.: Human Rights Watch, September 1996). See also Larry Diamond, Anthony Kirk-Greene, and Oyeleye Oyediran, eds., *Transition without End: Politics and Society under Babangida* (Boulder, Colo.: Lynne Rienner Publishers, 1997).

2. *New York Times*, December 7, 1997. The April 25 polls were reported by the PanAfrican News Agency (Lagos), April 26, 1998; and by Agence France-Presse (Lagos), April 26, 1998.

3. A more detailed account of political repression and the cases of detainees is provided in the report by Human Rights Watch/Africa, "Nigeria: Transition or Travesty? Nigeria's Endless Process of Return to Civilian Rule," *Human Rights Watch* 9, no. 6, (October 1997).

4. The deficiencies in the judicial process surrounding the Ogoni activists have been documented by the Civil Liberties Organization, based in Lagos, in its 1995 annual report. The UN secretary-general sent a fact-finding team to Nigeria in March and April 1996 to investigate the circumstances of the trial and executions. They found that the judicial process fell far short of accepted international standards. The group's report, submitted on April 23, is available as Annex I to UN Doc. A/50/960. See also Human Rights Watch/Africa, *Permanent Transition*, pp. 33–36.

5. The most prominent attacks include the killing of Alfred Rewane, a politician, businessman, and NADECO financier, in October 1995; a shooting in February 1996 that seriously wounded Alex Ibru, former interior minister in Abacha's first cabinet and publisher of the nation's leading independent newspaper, the *Guardian*; the killing of Kudirat Abiola, the outspoken first wife of Chief M. K. O. Abiola, in June 1996; a shooting attack on Chief Abraham Adesanya, a senior NADECO leader, in January 1997; the killing of Tokunbo Onagoruwa, son of Olu Onagoruwa, the former attorney general, in an apparent attack on his father in late 1996; and the shooting of journalist Tunde Oladepo in February 1998; no one was charged in any of these incidents.

6. This pamphlet has circulated among elites in the northern states since it was released in 1994. The document is attributed to the "Yoruba Solidarity Forum" and, in the classic format of conspiracy literature, supposedly reproduces confidential documents detailing the Yoruba plans. The pamphlet is entitled "The Master-Plan: The Agenda that Conquered IBB" (no locale), Yoruba Solidarity Forum, 1994. The document was brought to our attention by a well-connected northerner, who had received it through a prominent northern traditional ruler and a senior Nigerian diplomat.

7. Human Rights Watch/Africa, "Nigeria: Transition or Travesty?" p. 32.

8. *Financial Times*, December 23, 1997.

9. See the interview with Saidu Dogo, the secretary-general of the Christian Association of Nigeria, titled "Army Is Unfair to Christians," *The Week* (Lagos), September 8, 1997, pp. 24–25.

10. This phrase is also found in Federal Republic of Nigeria, *Second National Development Plan 1970–74* (Lagos: Federal Government Printer, 1970), p. 31.

11. On the phenomenon of competitive communalism, see Ernest J. Wilson III, *Politics and Culture in Nigeria*, Center for Political Studies, Institute for Social Research, University of Michigan, Ann Arbor, Michigan, 1988.

12. This term has been elaborated by Richard A. Joseph, *Democracy and Prebendal Politics in Nigeria: The Rise and Fall of the Second Republic* (Cambridge: Cambridge University Press, 1987).

13. Julius O. Ihonvbere, "Economic Crisis, Structural Adjustment and Social Crisis in Nigeria," *World Development* 21, no. 1 (January 1993).

14. *Human Rights Practices in Nigeria, July 1996–June 1997*, Constitutional Rights Project, Lagos, 1997, p. 32.

15. Agence France Presse (Lagos), December 24, 1997.

16. Pan African News Agency (Lagos), August 20, 1997.

17. Matthew Tostevin, "Oil Giant Shell Hit by Rash of Attacks in Nigeria," Reuters (Lagos), December 19, 1997; Matthew Tostevin, "Nigerian Villagers Shut Flow Stations," Reuters (Lagos), November 12, 1997.

18. Matthew Hassan Kukah, *Religion, Politics and Power in Northern Nigeria* (Ibadan: Spectrum, 1993).

19. The official voter register tallied almost 55 million eligible voters over the age of eighteen. In a developing country of 110 million people, with Nigeria's high growth rate, standard demographic estimates indicate that 48 percent of the population (about 50 million people) are under the age of fifteen. See World Bank, *World Development Report 1997* (Washington, D.C.: Oxford University Press for the World Bank, 1997), p. 220. In light of these demographic realities, it is likely that the official voters' rolls were substantially inflated in the March 1997 local government elections. Nigeria probably does not have 55 million citizens over the age of eighteen, and even if there were such numbers, 100 percent coverage in voter registration is implausible, given the evident administrative problems of reaching a poorly educated rural population.

▬ 5 ▬

1. Human Rights Watch/Africa, *Permanent Transition: Current Violations of Human Rights in Nigeria* (Washington, D.C.: Human Rights Watch, September 1996), p. 26.

2. "Head of Anglican Communion in Nigeria Calls for Seven Days of Fasting," Agence France-Presse (Lagos), December 28, 1997.

3. Matthew Tostevin, "Nigerian Christian Groups Amplify Democracy Call," Reuters (Lagos), May 18, 1998.

4. Important discussions of religion and politics in Nigeria can be found in Matthew Hassan Kukah, *Religion, Politics and Power in Northern Nigeria* (Ibadan: Spectrum Books, 1993), and Iheanyi Enwerem, *A Dangerous Awakening: The Politicization of Religion in Nigeria* (Ibadan: Institut Français de Recherche en Afrique, 1995).

5. We are grateful to Rev. William M. Howard, Jr., for elaborating on many of these connections.

— INDEX —